The Complete Guide to Crystal Astrology

360 crystals and sabian symbols for personal health, astrology and numerology

Marina Costelloe

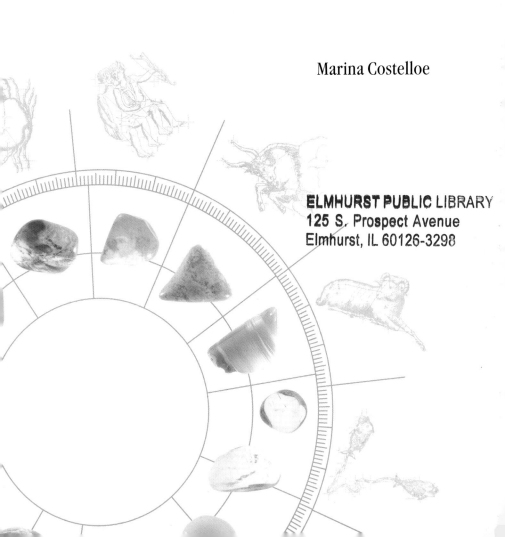

Publisher's note

All information in this book has been compiled according to the publisher's best knowledge and belief. People react in different ways however, and therefore neither the publisher nor the author can, for individual cases, provide a guarantee as to the effectiveness or harmlessness of the applications described herein. In cases of serious physical or mental health concerns, please consult a physician, alternative practitioner, or psychologist.

1 2 3 4 5 6 7 8 9 10 17 16 15 14 13 12 11 10 09 08 07

Marina Costelloe
The Complete Guide to Crystal Astrology

Copyright © Earthdancer GmbH 2007
Text Copyright © Marina Costelloe 2007
Key Words reprinted from *The Sabian Symbols In Astrology*, by Dr. Marc Edmund Jones
ISBN: 978-0-943358-40-6, with permission of: Aurora Press; P.O. Box 573, Santa Fe, N. M. 87504 USA
Healing Body Points reprinted from *A Handbook of Medical Astrology*, by Jane Ridder-Patrick
ISBN: 978-0-9551989-0-8, with permission of Jane Ridder-Patrick / CrabApple Press, Edinburgh 2006

First published in UK in 2007 by Earthdancer GmbH an imprint of :
Findhorn Press, 305a The Park, Findhorn, Forres IV36 3TE, Great Britain

Cover design: Dragon Design UK, images: Astrofoto, www.astrofoto.de
Editing: Claudine Bloomfield
Typeset in ITC Garamond condensed

Printed in China – 100% of the paper used for this book is sourced from responsibly managed forests

ISBN: 978-1-84409-103-4

This book is dedicated to the Crystal Children

Contents

An Introduction to Crystal Astrology

"As above, so below"

For millennia people have looked upward to the stars, interpreting patterns, cycles and symbols; and for as long, people have been looking below at birthstones and gemstones. Crystal Astrology unites and maps spiritual truth and guidance with the stars and the Crystal Elements. The power contained in our Crystal Elements enhances our native talents and attributes; it energises our life. "Crystal Astrology" is a completely new phrase in our spiritual vocabulary. It is a system whereby unique Crystal Elements are allocated to each degree of the zodiacal wheel – a unique energy assigned to each degree of the Zodiac, 360 different Crystal Elements.

Most people not only know their own star sign, they also know other people's star signs and what those signs mean astrologically. Have you ever noticed how another person can have the same star sign as you but be significantly different in personality? Have you ever wondered why? Traditional astrology explains much of why we are so different in that all the planets need to be taken into consideration, not just our star sign. Aspects, placement, cusps, houses, and all that 'technical jargon' go a long way to explaining those details. However, many of us never really get round to fully understanding traditional astrology. With *Crystal Astrology* we use Crystal Elements to explore these differences and details, as most of us can relate energetically to crystals in a more obvious way than we do to traditional astrological, mathematical listings.

Crystal Astrology follows the lead of the New Age ideal that we are now within the ascension process, and that we have a greater capacity to understand and a greater desire to know than ever before. Heightened awareness and experience show that in this age we need more than 12 simple, broad, astrological or zodiac sign interpretations – we can actually understand and take in 360 of them, 360 being the number of degrees in a wheel or circle.

Early in the book, we discuss how to use crystals in astrology, what the information means, and how best you can utilise it. We will explore Traditional and

Modern Birthstone Lore; Crystal Astrology; Astrological Numerology; Sabian Symbols and the corresponding key words from the astrologer Dr. Marc Edmund Jones' book, *The Sabian Symbols in Astrology*; Healing Body Points as listed by astrologer Jane Ridder-Patrick in her book, *A Handbook to Medical Astrology*; Crystal Expression; Crystal Message; Sun Focus and Crystal Affirmation. Together we will rediscover who you really are, using relevant sections in this book to transform your Natal Astrology Chart into a Crystal Astrology Chart.

But first, with a minimum of fuss you can look up *your birthday* and find out *your solar Crystal Element* and *Crystal Message*. The crystal element associated with your birthday is known as your *solar* Crystal Element because the crystal energy is linked to the specific degree of the sun when you were born. Your solar Crystal Element promotes personal power, good fortune, karmic direction, and abilities. For example, if your birthday is the 22nd of March then your solar Crystal Element is Orange Aventurine, and the Crystal Message includes jovial and merry emotions, optimism, self-confidence and enthusiasm. Also, look to the Crystal Elements and Crystal Messages directly before and after your solar Crystal Element and take notice of them – they play a fundamental role in who you are and indicate which crystal energies are available to you. Use the Crystal Message given with your birth date in *Crystal Astrology* to crystallise your life. You can also visit www.crystalastrology.com to find out your Crystal Elements.

Crystal Astrology has been waiting on the sidelines for some years now, waiting for the 'new' rocks and crystals to surface and become available, such as Tanzanite, Avalonite, Aqua Aura and Lemurian Seed Crystals. I would like to add that it is by no means necessary to try and obtain your Crystal Elements in their physical form, and that a great deal of benefit can be obtained from looking at a picture or touching a stone in a natural environment or museum. Some of the elements are difficult to acquire and may require a treasure hunt on your part. As you read on, you may well find that several Crystal Elements resonate with you, and it is my firm belief that the best Crystal Element for you will come to you if you are meant to work with it. The focus in Crystal Astrology is a positive one – look to the energy in each of the 360 Crystal Elements to support you in your personal ascension process. My hope is that you look at various Crystal Elements to see and feel how each is important in your life, and then use them to energise yourself.

Traditional and Modern Birthstones

Your solar Crystal Element works in powerful harmony with your traditional birthstone. Birthstones are believed to support a positive life, protect from harm, bring good fortune, and aid healing. It is a long-held belief that our birth stone or gem is lucky, and that the power of the gemstone enhances our native talents and attributes, and energises our life. Crystals and other valuable mineral kingdom gifts are used as talismans, amulets and birthstones. Many cultures and religions hold crystals in high regard, utilising them in religious services, garments, crowns, sceptres, orbs, swords, and rings, as personal adornment and to signify and amplify spiritual power.

One of the surviving birthstone traditions is attributed to the Hoshen Breastplate, which was written about in the book of Exodus. Along with a great deal of energy and power, the Hoshen Breastplate contained one precious gem for each of the 12 tribes of Israel: ruby, topaz, aquamarine, turquoise, sapphire, emerald, jacinth, agate, amethyst, chrysolite, onyx and jasper. Each stone served as an expression of faith and optimism within the spiritual community.

There are a variety of birthstone charts linking gemstones with calendar months. All of the various charts differ with tradition, age and culture. The modern birthstone list most commonly referred to is from the American National Association of Jewellers, and was adopted in 1912 . The Ayurvedic birthstone list is derived from Indian medicine and dates back to 1500 BC. Other birthstone lists also exist: traditional birthstone lists from various traditions and customs from the past 600 years; mystical birthstone lists of Tibetan origin that date back over a thousand years; and ancient birthstone lists also dating back over 1000 years for Arabic, Hebrew, Hindu and Roman belief systems. Planetary gemstone lists link particular crystals with planets, indicating that certain gemstones enhance the power of certain planetary influences in your life.

Zodiac Birthstones are linked with a zodiac sign instead of being associated with a calendar month. Zodiac Birthstone lists often cite up to five or more gemstones for each star sign and these lists vary. Table 1 is a cumulative list of modern, commonly-accepted zodiac birthstones.

Table 1. Zodiac Birthstones

Zodiac Sign	Dates	Birthstone
Aries	Mar. 21 – Apr. 20	Bloodstone, Diamond
Taurus	Apr. 21 – May 21	Sapphire, Amber, Emerald, Azurite
Gemini	May 22 – Jun. 21	Agate, Chrysoprase, Citrine, Moonstone, Pearl
Cancer	Jun. 22 – Jul. 22	Emerald, Moonstone, Pearl, Ruby
Leo	Jul. 23 – Aug. 23	Onyx, Carnelian, Sardonyx, Tourmaline
Virgo	Aug. 24 – Sep.22	Carnelian, Jade, Jasper, Sapphire
Libra	Sep. 23 – Oct. 23	Peridot, Lapis Lazuli, Opal
Scorpio	Oct. 24 – Nov. 22	Beryl, Apache Tear, Aquamarine, Topaz
Sagittarius	Nov. 23 – Dec. 21	Topaz, Amethyst, Ruby, Sapphire, Turquoise
Capricorn	Dec. 22 – Jan. 20	Ruby, Agate, Garnet, Black Onyx
Aquarius	Jan. 21 – Feb. 18	Garnet, Amethyst, Moss Agate, Opal
Pisces	Feb. 19 – Mar. 20	Amethyst, Aquamarine, Rock Crystal

There is even a birthstone allocated for the day of the week on which you were born, known as your day stones: Monday is Pearl; Tuesday is Garnet; Wednesday is Cat's Eye; Thursday is Emerald; Friday is Topaz; Saturday is Sapphire; and Sunday is Ruby.

Interestingly, there are also planet-metal affinities, that have been known for eons, and were added to after the discovery of the outer planets (Table 2). These metal-planet affinities are used in alchemy, homeopathy, and astrology. In *Crystal Astrology*, metals are included in the list of Crystal Elements.

Table 2. Planet – Metal Affinities

Age	Planet	Metal	Zodiac Sign
ANCIENT	Sun	Gold	Leo
	Moon	Silver	Cancer
	Mercury	Mercury	Gemini/Virgo
	Venus	Copper	Taurus/Libra
	Mars	Iron	Aries
	Jupiter	Tin	Sagittarius
	Saturn	Lead	Capricorn
MODERN	Uranus	Uranium	Aquarius
	Neptune	Neptunium	Pisces
	Pluto	Plutonium	Scorpio

Just as a traditional birthstone vibrates to a Zodiac Sign, the same is true for metals. Work with metals in your life in the same way you work with Birthstones.

Traditional and modern birthstones systems, and the variations within them, work. These systems provide a strong tone, a strong crystal presence in our lives. These birthstones resonate with broad-scale aspects in our life such as love, health, prosperity and protection. Many people resonate with divine affinity to their chosen birthstone. Birthstone lore is valuable to us, and has been for thousands of years, and we should always honour these traditions and incorporate them into our life. *Crystal Astrology* expands on this concept and lists 360 Crystal Elements to provide a more detailed and personal Crystal Element. The Crystal Elements should be considered a 'harmony' to the underlying strengths of traditional birthstone systems.

Crystal Astrology

'Crystallise your life'

How it works

- *Crystal Astrology* provides added insight into an individual astrology chart by allocating a Crystal Element to each and every degree in the astrological wheel.
- *Crystal Astrology* lets you look up your solar Crystal Element and helps redefine your natal astrology chart with crystal energy.

Crystal energy is unique energy, and everyone will vibrate uniquely to a given crystal type, and to varieties within a crystal type; no two stones are exactly the same to the sensitive crystal worker.

For each Crystal Element there is much traditional and modern information, but many writers concentrate this information to resonate with the chakra system or major aspects such as love, prosperity, healing or protection. Within *Crystal Astrology* I put forward a brief and distinctive analysis of each Crystal Element, presenting it in a simple and clear information sequence that resonates with the stone's attributes, but also assigns each stone an astrological point so that we can easily use them to learn and grow.

Let us start with traditional astrology, based on a circle and planet placement. There are 360 degrees in a circle, and therefore 360 degrees in an astrological wheel. We are all familiar with the 12 star signs of the zodiac, Aries through to Pisces; there are 12 segments in the circle, and with a little maths we calculate 30 degrees for each star sign of the zodiac.

- 360 degrees in a circle divided by 12 star signs = 30 degrees for each star sign
- One Crystal Element for each astrological degree
- 360 *DIFFERENT* Crystal Elements
- 30 *DIFFERENT* Crystal Elements for each star sign

So, for Aries there are 30 degrees of Aries and 30 Crystal Elements; 30 Crystal Elements for Taurus, and so on till we get to the end of the astrological wheel at Pisces.

Quick Crystal Astrology

Just by looking up your birthday, you can work out so much about yourself. For instance, if your birthday is April 2nd, simply look for your birthday in the book and you will see:
Birthdays: April 1st-April 3rd
Crystal Element: Sodalite

Sodalite is your Crystal Element Focus.

Born on February 9th, you will find:
Birthdays: February 7th-9th
Crystal Element: Schalenblende

Schalenblende is your Crystal Element Focus.

Your Focus is the Crystal Element that applies specifically to you.
Solar Crystal Element = Birthday Crystal Element = Focus

Reading through Crystal Astrology you may notice that your birth date does not link neatly to one Crystal Element. This is because there are 360 degrees in a circle, 360 Crystal Elements, but 365 days in a year, so your Crystal Element Focus depends on where you were born and at what time.

In the next section we will discuss how the Crystal Elements either side of your Focus are potent in Crystal Astrology, so even using the book as a quick reference guide will give you your significant Crystal Elements. But to accurately define which Crystal Element is your Focus, visit www.crystalastrology.com for your free, personalised Crystal Astrology report; or www.astro.com to obtain your free natal astrology report. You can, however, utilize this book without an astrological chart. More information about this is given in the Detailed Crystal Astrology section.

The Crystal Sequence

Karmic Condition   *Focus*   *Quest*

What tools do I have? How do I move forward? Where am I headed? These are the questions answered by the Crystal Sequence. As we have discussed, within Crystal Astrology you can look up your date of birth to obtain your Crystal Element Focus and its associated information. This crystal energy is the Focus of your abilities. But each degree holds so much potential, energy, description and consequence, you should always look to the Crystal Element directly before your Focus, known as your Karmic Condition, and the Crystal Element directly after, known as your Quest. The astrological information on either side of your Focus gives valuable insight into your astrology.

Karmic Condition is the mission you have set out on, and the tools you have available to you to succeed.
Focus is your strength and power source, your movement through life.
Quest sheds light onto the outcome and experience; it is the culmination of your efforts.

Example: Born on the 19th of August, your Crystal Element Focus is Rainbow Fluorite. Look to the Crystal Elements directly before and after the Crystal Element Focus to form your Crystal Sequence:

Karmic Condition	*Focus*	*Quest*
Desert Rose	Rainbow Fluorite	Citrine

You may be drawn to a significant Crystal Element in your Crystal Sequence and prefer to work with that crystal as a significant energy force in your life. In the body of the Crystal Astrology book you will find a significant amount of information: born on August 19th, there are three relevant sections, Leo 25, Leo 26 and Leo 27 (see below).

Karmic Condition

The astrological degree directly before the Focus degree is the Karmic Condition. The Karmic Condition provides valuable insight into what tools are available to you and what strengths you have. The Karmic Condition may also indicate past life memories, early history or "baggage", and it provides insight into the causes of certain traits and patterns. Leo 25 is the Karmic Condition for Leo 26.

Focus

For someone born on August 19th, Leo 26 is their sun Focus, the significant section that relates to this person's birthday. This section describes and lists the main symbols that this person should evaluate in their life. It offers the greatest gifts, and highlights subtle challenges. It provides a valuable summary of information pertaining to the individual's natal chart.

Quest

The Quest is the third part of the crystal sequence and is the astrological degree directly after the Focus, in this case Leo 27. The Quest offers insight into where you are headed, and information to assess purpose, possible outcomes and future potential.

Leo 26 is the degree at which your sun was sitting at the time of your birth. Leo 25 sheds extra light on your abilities and personality. Leo 27 helps you toward your future. This crystal sequence provides you with three potent Crystal Elements to exchange energy with, learn from, and work with. Choose the crystal from your crystal sequence that you are most attracted to, and honour the energy and support the other crystals have to offer you.

The brilliantly original concept of the sequence of Karmic Condition - Focus - Quest was defined by Lynda Hill, author and astrologer, and is regularly used as a tool in reading the Sabian Symbols. Kindly, Lynda Hill provided me with guidance and permission to transfer her Sabian Symbol Sequence definitions and methods to *Crystal Astrology*. Read more about Sabian Sequence in the Sabian Symbol section.

Detailed Crystal Astrology

Transforming your natal astrology chart into a Crystal Astrology chart

Fundamentally, *Crystal Astrology* substitutes a Crystal Element for a significant astrological degree in your natal chart. In the case of a birth chart, Western Astrology represents the positions of the planets and houses as seen from the place of birth at the time of birth. Western Astrology works in many other ways, including horary astrology, transits, progressions, solar arcs, secondary progressions. Since a crystal is allocated to a unique zodiacal degree, *Crystal Astrology* can be transferred to these other methods, but we will focus on Natal Charts – birth charts (Geocentric Tropical Zodiac Placidus Houses).

There are thousands of excellent Western Astrology books and courses to learn the fundamentals of Astrology; Crystal Astrology works within these guidelines by substituting a Crystal Element for each astrological degree – any astrology method can be transformed into a Crystal Astrology chart. However, briefly outlined here are some essentials of Astrology:

- Twelve star signs – Aries, Taurus, Gemini, Cancer, Leo, Virgo, Libra, Scorpio, Sagittarus, Capricorn, Aquarius and Pisces – indicate 12 broad personality energy types or drives.
- Planets, asteroids, nodes, etc., describe which energy is being expressed.
- Twelve houses, which are the segments in an astrology chart that direct us to where the energies of the planets and the energies of the star signs are active.

There are various methods, calculations and traditions involved in calculating an astrology chart. In Crystal Astrology, the Astrology Charts are calculated in the Geocentric longitude with Placidus houses, True Node system. Other methods include: Equal House, Whole Sign, Draconic, Koch, Regiomontanus, Porphyry, Topocentric, etc.

Your natal chart is a snapshot of where the planets, asteroids and more celestial bodies were at the time of your birth. Where your Sun was located in the sky defines your star sign. Astrological information is described in star sign, degrees and minutes notation. By going directly to www.crystalastrology.com you will be able to obtain your complete Crystal Astrology list.

Your Crystal Astrology listing becomes alive with crystal energy, colour and meaning. As with traditional astrology your SUN is your core, your solar centre, your powerhouse. The sun's significance in describing essentially who you are and how you are now becomes crystal clear. *Crystal Astrology* really deals with looking up your natal sun information. However, you can use this guide to completely transform your astrology chart into crystals. You can convert each planet's placement into crystal energy. Simply keep in mind the following guidelines:

The Moon - Emotions - Look to this Crystal Element to balance emotions.
Mercury - Communication - Look to this Crystal Element to enhance communication skills.
Venus - Love and relationships - Look to this Crystal Element to increase positive relationships.
Mars - Energy and motivation - Utilise this Crystal Element to move forward in life.
Jupiter - Career, luck and abundance - Look to this Crystal Element for success.
Saturn - Learning and experience - Choose this Crystal Element to help bring rewards.
Uranus - Unexpected gifts and talents - Utilise this Crystal Element to make the most out of every situation.
Neptune - Psychic and spiritual talents - Meditate on this Crystal Element energy to open new doors.
Pluto - Transformation - Look to this Crystal Element to guide you through rough times.
Chiron - Healing themes - Ask this Crystal Element to promote health and wellbeing.
North Node - Karmic Future - Talents we develop in this life.
South Node - Karmic History - Talents we bring into this life.

The North and South Nodes of the Moon are mathematically calculated points where the Moon's orbit intersects the plane of the ecliptic. The North and South Nodes are opposite each other; these two points act as signposts for our personal karmic journey. The most influential energies apart from your Sun are the North Node and South Node (North Node + South Node = LIFE PATH), and Jupiter. The Moon's Nodes and Jupiter are truly powerful when making life decisions.
Let us look at an example of a specific astrological natal chart:
So your birthday is the 2nd of April, 1974; your natal sun is then sitting at Aries 12 degrees 33 minutes - we round the minutes up to the whole degree

making Aries 13, and your Sun Crystal Element is Sodalite. You can change all of the longitude points into Crystal Elements, creating a Crystal Astrology chart.

Just to clarify, when transforming your astrological data into Crystal Astrology, round up the degree to the nearest whole number; from the above example: Moon Leo 11, Venus Aquarius 26, Mars Gemini 20, and so on. Always round up the minutes to the next whole degree regardless of the number of minutes, unlike in mathematics, because the zodiac starts at 00.00 degrees, and the Sabian Symbols start at 1.00 degree. So, to continue our example:

Natal Chart
Birthday: April 2nd 1974, Time 3:30pm
Sydney NSW Australia 33S52 151E13 (Time: Zone AEST -10:00)

Point	Longitude	Whole Degree	Crystal Element
Sun	12° Aries 05'57"	Aries 13	Sodalite
Moon	10° Leo 33'12"	Leo 11	Tree Agate
Mercury	16° Pisces 08	Pisces 17	Yellow Apatite
Venus	25° Aquarius 42	Aquarius 25	Vanadium Beryl
Mars	19° Gemini 18	Gemini 20	Green Kyanite
Saturn	28° Gemini 48	Gemini 29	Hessonite
Uranus	26° Libra 20 R	Libra 27	Black Hypersthene
Neptune	09° Sagittarius 30 R	Sagittarius 10	Yellow Sapphire
Pluto	05° Libra 17 R	Libra 6	Lazulite
North Node	22° Sagittarius 13 R	Sagittarius 23	Blue Chalcedony
South Node	22° Gemini 13 R	Gemini 23	Green Quartz
Chiron	19° Aries 51	Aries 20	Rhodochrosite

R = Retrograde, which can be interpreted as the need for the support of this Crystal Element in your life.

You have the power to take, transform and understand each Crystal Element as it personally influences you. Your Crystal Astrology chart is an important guide to self-discovery. There are endless opportunities for interpretation and use of the Crystal Elements including relationship synastry, progressed charts, karmic strengths, soul's purpose, life path, past lives, and karmic contracts. Once you know your Crystal Elements, the associated information contained in each section will appear in your life in many ways. That knowledge will support you.

Information you will find in this book

There are 360 sections in this book, one for each astrological degree, divided into 12 sections that correspond to star signs. Crystal Astrology offers a modern tool to help us map our spiritual potential using a multi-disciplinary approach. Crystal Astrology provides information for an individual to use to transform and understand their unique talents in the moment, and as a guide to self-discovery. Let us look at an example of a section for a birthday on the 19th of February.

Pisces 1
Birthdays: February 18th-19th
Numerology: 331
Sabian Symbol: A public marketplace
Marc Edmund Jones Key Word: Commerce
Jane Ridder-Patrick Healing Body Point: Right calcaneum
Crystal Element: Silver (native)
Expression: Elemental silver is a naturally occurring metal. Silver promotes trust, excellence, balance, and the attraction and retention of wealth. It is an alchemical metal.
Message: Efficient allocation of resources enhances the positive flow of wealth.
Sun Focus: You value everyone and everything, seeing energy exchange as vital.
Affirmation: I am prosperous in my endeavours.

The following sections look at each subtitle in detail:

Astrological Degree

The Astrological Degree is essentially the title for each section and lists an astrological sign and a number, for example:

Pisces 1

Astrological Degrees are mathematical calculations labelling significant positions, of planets for example, when creating an astrology chart. The fundamental premise utilises the mathematical concept that a circle has 360 degrees. This subsection, then, indicates the astrological degree (rounded up to the full degree) and is unique for each section, starting with Aries 1 and listing the 360 degrees to Pisces 30.

Birthdates

The second subtitle in each section provides a range of birthdates, generated from reading an ephemeris. For example:

Birthdays: February 18th-19th

If your birthday falls within these dates this is one of your solar Crystal Elements, and it may be your *Focus* depending on the location and time of your birth (as discussed in the Detailed Astrology section).

You will notice in each section a couple of days are listed; this is because there are more than 360 days in a calendar year. Also, your place and time of birth influences the Astrological Degree of your Sun.

Astrological Numerology

Astrological Numerology lists the number of the corresponding Astrological Degree. For example:

Numerology: 331

Astrological Numerology therefore is a unique and sequential number between 1 and 360. Aries 1 has the Astrological Numerology of 1 and Pisces 30 has the Astrological Numerology of 360. Astrological Numerology is not the same as name numerology however; name numerology is explained within this section for the benefit of those who are interested.

In *Crystal Astrology* an additional level is added to the traditional name reduced numerology base of 1-11. By looking at the sacred geometry of a circle and accepting that each number between 1 and 360 holds a specific energy pattern or energetic space, we can access potent information in the astrology chart and crystal energy. Astrological numerology increases our awareness, knowledge and understanding to 360.

Within *Crystal Astrology* the Astrological Numerology for Amethyst is placed in harmony with Sagittarius 30, Astrological Numerology number 270, Sagittarius 30 being the 270th degree in the Astrological Wheel. The Astrological Numerology of Amethyst is 270; Amethyst vibrates to the Sabian Symbol of the Pope blessing the faithful, and the key word is 'sanctity', therefore the number 270 holds the energy of 'sanctity'.

Within *Crystal Astrology* the Astrological Numerology for Black Obsidian vibrates to the key word 'realisation', and the number 1. The last Crystal Element in *Crystal Astrology* vibrates to Astrological Number 360, the keyword is 'discernment', and Gneiss is the stone.

Astrological Numerology offers new, subtle numerology meanings that can be utilised with crystals and other important information such as names, addresses, repetitive number patterns, time, and astrology where numbers greater than 11 are generated. You can use *Crystal Astrology* as a numerology reference book: notice a number 182 – a street number, a registration number – and look it up; it is Moldavite energy and you will find valuable insight within section 182.

Name Numerology is very different to Astrological Numerology. In Name Numerology, crystal workers have attributed a single number significance to crystals and minerals based on each crystal's name. Crystals have been numerologically assessed due to the name of a crystal in a given language. Crystal names were converted into numbers, and then reduced using a 1-11 system. Here we will look at Amethyst and detail its Name Numerology rather than its Astrological Numerology. Using a conversion table (Table 3) and the name, we work out a crystal's name numerology:

Table 3. *The name numerology conversion table*

1 2 3 4 5 6 7 8 9
A B C D E F G H I
J K L M N O P Q R
S T U V W X Y Z

A+M+E+T+H+Y+S+T
1+ 4+ 5+2+8+ 7+1+2 = 30   *3+0 = 3*

Amethyst has a reduced name numerology value of 3 (self expression) and, as discussed above, an Astrological Numerology of 270 (sanctity). The method of single number name numerology is powerful and it works; it is very useful in many circumstances. The energy of single number name numerology should never be underestimated. Keep in mind that name numerology is subject to change, depending on spellings and names in different languages. Astrological Numerology is determined by the Crystal Element, even if it is defined differently in various languages or cultures. Astrological Numerology provides a framework for advanced numerology. Astrological Numerology reinforces the uniqueness of each individual Crystal Element by associating the numbers 1 to 360 with Crystal Element definitions, and Sabian Symbol meanings, aiding in the individual ascension process.

Recommended Reading:
Drayer, Ruth. *Numerology: The Power in Numbers*, U.S.A., Square One Publishers, 2002.

Sabian Symbol

For each astrological degree, there is a Sabian Symbol. For example:

Sabian Symbol: A public marketplace

The Sabian Symbols were delivered into our reality by the astrologer Marc Edmund Jones, and clairvoyant Elsie Wheeler, in 1922. The Sabian symbols are a unique set of 360 descriptive, symbolic images, derived from an ancient

Mesopotamian source through a channelling session. Sabian Symbols are most commonly used as a guide in interpretative astrology and oracle divination. There is one Sabian Symbol for each of the 360 astrological degrees, therefore one for each Crystal Element, and therefore one for each astrological numerology section. The suggested reading list at the end of this section will lead you to uncover amazing Sabian Symbol truths.

Sabian Symbols shed light on who we are, where we belong, and how to succeed. Each Sabian Symbol is understood from the perspective of our own individual life experience, which allows us to access detailed information about our own expression in this world. Within our personal astrology chart, Sabian Symbols are our essence. Individualised interpretation is the beauty of the Sabian Symbols - you have the power to take, transform and understand each symbol as it personally influences you; you can choose to take it to the depths and heights of interpretation.

Let's try and explain what the symbols are, and how they work.

Let's light up some famous people's SUN Sabian Symbols, their Focus symbols, with some strong imagery and a brief interpretation. These people all harness this solar energy to help power them through life. See a new side to these famous people:

Bill Gates' SUN Sabian Symbol is Scorpio 6 'A gold rush'. Indeed Bill Gates has not only found gold, but has also helped many other people gain wealth by finding the gold mine in computers, and in his personal endeavours to assist those less fortunate than himself. Bill Gates donates billions of dollars to various charities.

Madonna's is Leo 23 'A yogi with transcendent powers yet untidy & unkempt'. Madonna rules her body, mind and spiritual self with extreme states of fitness and religious pursuits, as a yogi does. This is her key to success, tapping into the power of her SUN sign and letting it help her with her 'self' goals.

In the same way you place crystals, you can place and interpret Sabian Symbols in your natal astrology chart with each planet, as in Traditional Astrology. The Sabian Symbols provide the fundamental framework to link Crystal Elements to Astrological Degrees.

Recommended Reading:

Jones, Dr. Marc Edmund. *The Sabian Symbols in Astrology: A Symbol Explained for Each Degree of the Zodiac*, Santa Fe, Aurora Press, 1993.

Hill, Lynda. *360 Degrees of Wisdom: Charting Your Destiny with the Sabian Oracle*, U.S.A., Plume Books, 2004.

Birkbeck, Lyn. *The Astrological Oracle: Divining Your Future and Resolving Your Past*, Great Britain, Thorsons, 2002.

Bovee, Blain. *Sabian Symbols & Astrological Analysis: The Original Symbols Fully Revealed*, U.S.A., Llewellyn Publications, 2004.

Key Word

This subsection lists the Key Word associated with the relevant Sabian Symbol, as defined by Dr Marc Edmund Jones and published in *The Sabian Symbols in Astrology*. The Key Words formulated by Dr Jones provide precious detail for the interpretation of the Sabian Symbols and Crystal Elements. There are 360 Key Words listed, each fundamentally defining an Astrological Degree with a specific essence. This is a unique key word, and energetically links the Astrological Numerology and the Crystal Element. An example for this section:

Marc Edmund Jones Key Word: Commerce

I was deeply honoured to be given permission by Aurora Press to utilise Dr Marc Edmund Jones' 360 Key Words from *The Sabian Symbols in Astrology: A Symbol Explained for Each Degree of the Zodiac* (Aurora Press. 1993),

Marc Edmund Jones' Key Words act as a signpost to show our strengths and talents; we can meditate on these words to see how they can help us attain a fulfilling life using the talents bestowed to us.

Healing Body Point

The Healing Body Point is one of 360 body parts as published by Jane Ridder-Patrick in *A Handbook of Medical Astrology*. An example for this section:

Jane Ridder-Patrick Healing Body Point: Right calcaneum

With the kind permission of Jane Ridder Patrick, I have included the body part that corresponds to each degree of the zodiac. The initial investigation into the 360 body parts was listed in the work of Elsbeth and Reinhold Ebertin, which appeared in "Anatomische Entsprechungen der Tierkreisgrade" [Anatomical Correspondences of the Zodiac Degrees] in 1949. Within Crystal Astrology I have used the body parts listed in Jane's must-read book, A Handbook of Medical Astrology (2nd edition, revised & expanded).

The healing body points are 360 parts of the human body that correspond to each of the 360 degrees in the astrological wheel. When looking up your Natal Astrology, you may find the associated body points are either physically, emotionally or spiritually particularly strong or particularly weak. To have this detail is useful when working with past-life trauma, childhood trauma, and for future reference.

If you find you have strengths or weaknesses in the body parts that correspond to the sun and planets in your chart, you can work at balancing them on a physical and energetic level. For example, we can choose any significant astrological placement here – your Moon, Sun, Saturn – but I will choose the South Node as, in my experience, it often reflects a health issue. If your South Node is Virgo 21 degrees 33 minutes, you round up the degree to 22 degrees which gives you the following information:

Virgo 22
Birthdays: September 13th-15th
Numerology: 172
Sabian Symbol: A royal coat of arms
Marc Edmund Jones Key Word: Prerogative
Ridder-Patrick Healing Body Point: Gall-bladder
Crystal Element: Blue Sapphire

Indicators to consider when interpreting this information:

- energetic issues relating to your gall bladder in this life or past lives
- intolerance to certain foods, digestion problems
- solar plexus issues
- looking at the Sabian Symbol information a genetic predisposition to certain hereditary illnesses

Blue sapphire, therefore, is the Crystal Element to which to attune your healing frequency. Please keep in mind it is not always essential to have the Crystal Element on the physical plane; you can have a picture, or hold its energy in your mind's eye.

It appears that enlightened souls who came here to tidy up a lot of karma, learn many lessons and help others learn about spirit have most of the planet corresponding Healing Body Parts on the weaker side. I feel this is a part of the lightworker's path.

Recommended Reading:
Ridder-Patrick, Jane. *A Handbook of Medical Astrology,* (2nd edition, revised & expanded), Edinburgh, CrabApple Press, 2006.

Crystal Element

In this section you will find a Crystal Element for each astrological degree. The interpretative information for each Crystal Element is found in the Expression, Message, Sun Focus and Affirmation sections that follow it. An example for this section:

Crystal Element: Silver

I have been working with crystals since 1991, and reading Sabian Symbols since 1993. I will often prescribe a crystal to help someone understand their Sabian Symbols, move through blocks in their life, and enhance their native abilities.

I realised a long time ago that crystal energy worked with astrology in a comprehensive way. I have incorporated various elements that include minerals, gems, metals, elements from the periodic table, rocks and stones – gifts of the mineral kingdom that can be acquired with thoughtful environmental awareness, gifts now known as the Crystal Elements. The word 'crystal' – as defined in most if not all New Age books including those written by Gienger, Hall and Melody – embraces natural crystals, rocks, stones, shells, opals, amber, minerals, periodic table elements, gemstones, metals, synthetic (man-made) or enhanced crystals, gemstones, and refined metals. Please note: dangerous and environmentally sensitive mineral kingdom gifts such as uranium, arsenic, coral and ivory are not included in the list.

It became obvious to me which Crystal Element went with which degree of the zodiac through studying the Sabian Symbols.

Allocating the best Crystal Element to each of the astrological degrees was the most important aspect of this work. I realised that the Crystal Element would have to harmonise with the already established system of Sabian Symbol Astrology. In a mutually supportive way then, the Sabian Symbols and Crystal Elements work together. Some obvious examples of corresponding Sabian Symbols and Crystal Elements that initiated this study include:

Aries 9   Sabian Symbol: A crystal gazer
              Crystal Element: Quartz Crystal

Taurus 30   Sabian Symbol: A peacock parading on a lawn
              Crystal Element: Peacock Ore

Scorpio 6   Sabian Symbol: A gold rush
              Crystal Element: Gold in Quartz

Another example of how this process worked for the other not-so-obvious Sabian Symbols is included for Cancer 22:

Cancer 22
Birthdays: July 13th-15th
Numerology: 112
Sabian Symbol: A woman awaiting a sailboat
Marc Edmund Jones Key Word: Equanimity
Jane Ridder-Patrick Healing Body Point: Gastric mucosa

Crystal Element: Avalonite

Expression: Avalonite is a trademark name for a natural, coral-peach zoisite. Avalonite supports freedom and unconditional love, and promotes earth healing.

Why Avalonite is linked with Cancer 22:

- The Sabian symbol for Cancer 22 is (on many levels) interpreted as a woman awaiting a sailboat. On a higher level we can interpret this as a lady of Avalon waiting for the boat to cross.
- Avalonite resonates woman, female energy, water, goddess. Avalon has a strong tone of love and wisdom.
- A wonderfully attractive stone, ripples of energy cross the surface and penetrate deeper and deeper into emotion and spirit.
- 22 is a Master Number – the energy of Avalonite is equivalent to a high energy number vibration.
- The people who have this astrological degree significantly in their chart have a fear of being loved, or have been hurt by a partner and feel they have been kept from fulfilling their destiny in some way because of that relationship; Avalonite heals this pain.

I discussed the above rationale with Kellie the Crystal Deva who was blessed to have discovered and named this Crystal Element – she agreed that Cancer 22 captures the essence of Avalonite.

Expression

The Expression section contains first a geological description, and second a metaphysical description of each Crystal Element. An example for this section:

Expression: Elemental silver is a naturally occurring metal. Silver promotes trust, excellence, balance, and the attraction and retention of wealth. It is an alchemical metal.

The Expression has a two-fold role. First, the Expression provides a simple geological description of the Crystal Element. The technical information is given for those who may be interested in the chemistry of the mineral, its formation, or use. A metaphysical description of the Crystal Element is then provided; this description is an extension of crystal descriptions provided by other authors, and specifically resonates with each Sabian Symbol, and in turn each Key Word and a unique Astrological Degree. The distinctive information contained within *Crystal Astrology* distinguishes one Crystal Element's attributes from another's.

The Expression section is succinctly written specifically to allow space for individual crystal energy experiences. I suggest you handle various crystals and read a variety of crystal literature, such as in the suggested reading list, to deepen your appreciation of crystal energy. Further study of crystals will bring you to a greater understanding, particularly in regards to how they resonate with the chakra system, how crystals work, and how to work with them.

By meditating on a certain crystal energy, you can help manifest, protect and energise your life. The wearing of crystals energises, and potentially promotes healing for your body, mind and spirit.

Recommended Reading:
Gienger, Michael. *Healing Crystals, The A-Z Guide to 430 Gemstones*, Italy, Earthdancer, 2005.
Melody. *Love is in the Earth, a Kaleidoscope of Crystals*, Wheat Ridge, Colorado., Earth-Love Publishing, 1995.
Cunningham, Scott.. *Cunningham's Encyclopedia of Crystal, Gem & Metal Magic*, Minnesota, Llewellyn Publications, 2002.

Message

The Crystal Element energy, and in most cases the linking Sabian Symbol image, often has extra information to impart in addition to the metaphysical properties. This extra information, which can be found in the "Message" subsection, clarifies the energy of the astrological degree and, of course, provides details on the energy of each specific Crystal Element. For example:

Message: Efficient allocation of resources enhances the positive flow of wealth.

The Message summary is not only useful in defining an astrological degree or Crystal Element energy, but also acts as a signpost for individuals to utilise in normal crystal work. The Message will help spiritually confirm life path choices, indicate skills needed in decision making, and illuminate the healing properties of Crystal Elements even if they are not in your personal astrology chart. When you are drawn to a particular crystal in your daily life, you can use Crystal Astrology as a quick reference guide to gain more insight into the energy of the crystal.

Crystal Elements can be used to enhance a specific symbol in your life, maybe angel energy, business skills, dexterity, romantic or unconditional love. You can meditate on or acquire the Crystal Element that corresponds to a favourable Sabian Symbol image, thereby drawing that energy into your life. For example, to invite Angelic Energy you could work with Euclase or Angelite.

Sun Focus

The Sun Focus is a positive and brief personality description if this astrological degree is your natal sun degree. For example:

Sun Focus: You value everyone and everything, seeing energy exchange as vital.

A star sign (30 degrees of the Astrology Wheel) provides a broad, sweeping description of native traits. The Sun Focus gives one particular aspect of your personality, providing a spiritual mirror to your higher self, opening the doors to a new, bright self-image.

The Sun Focus is our essence. The corresponding crystal energy helps us meditate on ourselves, our purpose and our life, with support and love. My hope is that you can use your Sun Focus as an important guide to self-discovery. When you see aspects from your Sun Focus in your life, they are like signposts along your life's path, showing you the way.

It is true that some people are more sensitive and attuned to crystal energies; if in doubt about your Focus Crystal Element consult a crystal worker. Keep in mind that with practice and exposure to crystals your skills will grow - your intuition and personal crystal interconnectivity will crystallise. You may feel drawn to tumbled stones, native crystals, cut stones, carved stones, naturally worn, or collective Crystal Elements. Use your intuition to assess which crystal forms you prefer and through them endeavour to learn more about yourself. Using your own in-built guidance system and universal energy patterns, you will come to accept and appreciate your unique talents and gifts, using both the information in this book and traditional astrology.

Affirmation

An affirmation is a tool to help connect us with the Crystal Element energy, for example:

Affirmation: I am prosperous in my endeavours.

The affirmations listed can be utilised in meditation, manifesting, earth healing, protection, acceptance and surrender. You can use the affirmation with or without its corresponding Crystal Element in a physical form; often a picture, a card, a thought can raise your energy to a Crystal Element's vibration.

Positive affirmations can change our lives; there is great power in prayer and positive thought. You may like to add to or change certain affirmations in this book; in particular you may like to add your name into an affirmation to make it more personal. Repetition is very important with affirmations: repeat the chosen affirmation often, in words, thought, writing, singing and art. Use the Crystal Element and/or Sabian Symbol image to help you visualise the positive intention.

When you are drawn to a certain crystal in the book, in nature, in a shop, or elsewhere, have a quick look at the associated affirmation and see how well it fits with what you really need to bring into your life.

How to use Crystal Astrology

Crystal Astrology Applications

Colour Therapy

You may notice a particular colour or theme recurs in your Crystal Astrology. Many of your Crystal Elements may be white, pink or green. Many of your Crystal Elements may be metallic indicating a refined chart, alchemically powerful. Other patterns may emerge; for instance, you may have a significant number of one type of rock, indicating strengths in your chart:

- Igneous rocks indicate power and clarity
- Sedimentary rocks indicate empathy and kindness
- Metamorphic rocks indicate complexity and durability

You can work with the dominant colour scheme in your Crystal Astrology Chart in the same way you can work with colour therapy in aura integration and chakra balancing. Here is a brief summary of the meaning of colours:

Table 4. Colour Interpretation Information

Colour	Chakra	Key Words
Red	Root	Energy and passion
Orange	Sacrum	Joy and creativity
Yellow	Solar Plexus	Personal power, intelligence
Green	Heart	Prosperity, harmony
Blue	Throat	Communication
Indigo	Third Eye	Intuition
Violet	Crown	Divine
White		Purity, wisdom
Black		Power, force
Coral/Peach		Love, harmony
Gold		Alchemy

Colour	Chakra	Key Words
Silver		Mirror, grace
Pink		Gentleness, love
Turquoise		Communication

You might like to place a tick next to the colours you have already identified in your Crystal Astrology to see if one colour is more significant that the others.

Many crystals including sapphires, diamonds, agate and carnelian may be colour enhanced to improve their colour and appeal. My personal experience is that colour enhancement to various crystals does not alter their innate properties, though it undoubtedly makes that mineral more appealing to some people. Colour enhancement boosts a crystal's potency in colour therapy, aura integration and chakra balancing in some people, and not in others.

Be completely aware of the Crystal Elements you own or purchase – find out if the Crystal Element is completely natural, enhanced in some way, or man-made. It is up to you to see how Crystal Elements work in your life. I know some crystal workers who only work with natural crystals and others who work with success using with a wide variety of enhanced, man-made, natural, and/or polished Crystal Elements.

Creating jewellery may be a unique and energising way to realise your crystal astrology. For thousands of years people have adorned themselves with beautiful Crystal Elements, and this continues today.

There are those significant times in life when a gift of a special piece of jewellery makes an enormous difference; for instance, during child birth a birthing bracelet or necklace might be given, or in times of stress or grief a simple heartfelt gift of jewellery can change a person's stamina, endurance and outlook. Crystallise your lives, and help others crystallise their life too.

Oracle

There are many uses for the *Crystal Astrology* book apart from astrological applications. The Crystal Elements are a modern tool for divining fortune, and the insights are truly astounding. By using *Crystal Astrology* as an Oracle you have the power in your own hands – you will receive crystal clear information, and it will be up to you to accept or reject the advice given.

Here are a few ways you can use *Crystal Astrology* as an oracle:

- Choose a number between 1 and 360 (using any method) and use *Crystal Astrology* as a look-up guide.
- Make your own Crystal Element List, cutting out each element to make 360 'cards' to choose from at random.
- If you have access to astrology software and a good knowledge of astrology, you can cast an Astrology chart for the moment (Horary) and interpret the details using *Crystal Astrology*.

Another way to use this book as an oracle is that when you see a sign, a house number, a large coloured pebble on the beach, a picture, hear a certain song playing everywhere you go - something that grabs your attention, something that keeps repeating in you life - use Crystal Astrology as a means to look-up and interpret the sign the universe is providing. Use this book as a reference guide. Use the various sections as a reference or index, looking up the Astrological Numerology for number signs, Crystal Elements for crystal signs, Sabian Symbols for words and images, and Healing Body Points for areas on the body.

If you have a question that needs answering or illuminating, the 360 Crystal Elements can provide insight and clear interpretations. Here's an example:

Question: What would people reading this book most like to know?
Method of choosing the outcome: randomly opening the book and pointing to a passage, in this case Number 71.

Gemini 11
Numerology: 71
Sabian Symbol: Newly opened lands offer the pioneer new opportunities
Marc Edmund Jones Key Word: Identification
Crystal Element: Tsavorite
Expression: Tsavorite is a green garnet, rich in vanadium and chromium. Traditionally, Tsavorite is a source of illumination for physical and spiritual growth.
Message: A fresh start, new beginnings, nourishing all stages of spiritual evolution.
Affirmation: I see great opportunities born from simplicity.

I would interpret the answer to be: The thing that people reading this book would most like to know is that it is an original source of illumination and growth.

The Crystal Children

The Crystal Children are a group of people, the majority of them born after 1996, whose auras are opalescent, pinky blue; they come here already talking about past lives, energy fields, chakras, stars, crystals and rocks, and are very concerned with love, peace and healing. This crystal nature starts to show itself explicitly as early as in the womb. Looking at a Crystal Child's birth chart using Crystal Astrology can provide insight into their exceptional traits.

I see a striking group feature for the period of time that most Crystal Children chose to be born, and that is a strong presence of Aquarius in their chart, particularly Uranus and Neptune in Aquarius. Keeping in mind that Uranus indicates advanced ideas, scientific discovery and the unexpected, and Neptune indicates specific psychic and spiritual abilities, both giant planets are bringing in and focusing Aquarius energy in these children. Many Crystal Children born in this period of time will also have an Aquarius Sun; an Aquarius moon; Aquarius Rising; Mercury, Venus, and/or Mars in their chart, all increasing the Aquarian influence in their lives.

You can look at the 30 Sabian Symbols and Crystal Elements for Aquarius within this book to see the trend that predicted this wave of children, and to help us as parents, family, friends and teachers of these children to understand some of their uniqueness.

The Key Words for these symbols include: Therapy, Courtesy, Progression, Affirmation, Accomplishment, Probity, Analysis, Concern, Approbation, Conviction, Clearance, Refinement, Aptitude, Serenity, Uniqueness, Efficiency, Tradition, Immediacy, Emanation, Continuity, Dramatization, Defiance, Durability, Ecstasy, Essentiality, Subtlety, Impact and Indication. These are all Aquarian traits, with specific Sabian Images to assist with each subtle expression of a Crystal Child's astrology and gifts.

The main parts of the body that correspond to these Sabian Symbols include the renal system, kidneys, bladder, right fibula, vascular system of skin, left calf muscle, left cruciate ligaments, and the spinal nervous system. This list may give insight to generational health strengths and challenges, and can be used in energetic healings.

Do you have a Crystal Person in your life that radiates the Sabian Symbol of a Hindu healer (Aquarius 4) or a Large White Dove bearing a message (Aquarius 20)? Whichever Sabian Symbols and Crystal Elements your Crystal Children chose when they were born are perfectly suited to them, and to the times in which they chose to incarnate.

Summary

Crystal Astrology helps us use crystal energy to access our own inner wisdom through details, images, feelings, colour, as well as crystal vibrations. We walk the pathway of deeper understanding by looking to all knowledge available to us, thereby gaining higher awareness and strengthening our connection with the universal consciousness.

Take time working with your Crystal Elements; realise the unique and beautiful energy that is in each and every Crystal Element. With eternal perspective both the diamond and the river pebble have magical potential. Meditate on your Crystal Elements; see how they appear in your life; look for them in your surroundings; search for more detail about your personal Crystal Elements, seeking crystal lore from other sources as well, and integrate the knowledge gleaned from your discoveries into your life. Always remember that crystal energy and universal energy are interconnected - use your crystal connections wisely, with love and compassion, in all ways, for the good of all.

ARIES 1
Birthdays: March 20th-22nd

Numerology: 1

Sabian Symbol: A woman rises out of the water, a seal embraces her.

Marc Edmund Jones Key Word: Realization

Jane Ridder-Patrick Healing Body Point: Cerebrum

Crystal Element: Obsidian

Expression: Obsidian is a shiny, black-green-grey volcanic glass. Obsidian is a protective, shielding stone; it opens opportunities and invites Mermaid Energy into your life.

Message: Knowledge is channelled from the unconscious to reality.

Sun Focus: Unique and independent, you display a high degree of psychic and creative talent.

Affirmation: I provide comfort through awareness.

ARIES 2
Birthdays: March 21st-23rd

Numerology: 2

Sabian Symbol: An entertaining comedian

Marc Edmund Jones Key Word: Release

Jane Ridder-Patrick Healing Body Point: Midbrain

Crystal Element: Orange Aventurine

Expression: Orange Aventurine is quartzite with hematite . Orange Aventurine amplifies jovial and merry emotions, firing up optimism. It echoes the Fool tarot card.

Message: Charismatic entertainer, satirical and ironic, energising.

Sun Focus: Self-confidence and enthusiasm are energised through comedy, lifting the emotions of those around you.

Affirmation: I laugh often with others.

ARIES 3

Birthdays: March 22nd-24th

Numerology: 3

Sabian Symbol: A cameo profile in the outline of his country

Marc Edmund Jones Key Word: Exploitation

Jane Ridder-Patrick Healing Body Point: Cerebellum

Crystal Element: Black Onyx

Expression: Black Onyx is a variety of quartz often used to create cameos. Onyx helps with the challenges in life, eliminating excess and releasing unnecessary energies.

Message: Face-to-face contact enhances clarity, empathy, comprehension and understanding.

Sun Focus: Whether politics, government or committee, heading different organizations becomes a prominent aspect of your life; lead the way.

Affirmation: I cooperate with people face-to-face.

ARIES 4

Birthdays: March 23rd-25th

Numerology: 4

Sabian Symbol: Two lovers strolling along a secluded walk

Marc Edmund Jones Key Word: Enjoyment

Jane Ridder-Patrick Healing Body Point: Pineal Gland

Crystal Element: Chrysoprase

Expression: Chrysoprase is a vibrant green variety of quartz. Chrysoprase brings good fortune, prosperity, and happiness-enhancing friendships. Echoes the Lover's tarot card energy.

Message: Learning to trust others and ourselves, we grow secure in relationships.

Sun Focus: You show others the opening of your heart, energising and expressing love with equality and balance.

Affirmation: I appreciate balance through love.

ARIES 5

Birthdays: March 24th-26th

Numerology: 5

Sabian Symbol: A triangle with golden wings

Marc Edmund Jones Key Word: Zeal

Jane Ridder-Patrick Healing Body Point: Both eyes

Crystal Element: Herkimer Diamond

Expression: A double-terminated quartz is known as a Herkimer Diamond. Herkimer Diamond promotes strong and clear meditation, astral travelling, and aids in past-life memory recall.

Message: Generates a heightened perspective, fulfilling understanding.

Sun Focus: You focus clear energies from the divine into life, allowing expansion through change.

Affirmation: I achieve spiritual enthusiasm through sensitive experiences.

ARIES 6

Birthdays: March 25th-27th

Numerology: 6

Sabian Symbol: A square, brightly lit on one side.

Marc Edmund Jones Key Word: Set

Jane Ridder-Patrick Healing Body Point: Eye Socket, orbital cavity

Crystal Element: Galena

Expression: Galena is a cubic lead mineral. Galena provides confidence to see through personal darkness, and the realisation that there is more than empty space – there is divine order.

Message: Promoting harmony and balance with a grounding, structured undertone.

Sun Focus: You act as a focus for healing and spiritual form in the world; people turn to you in their time of need.

Affirmation: I seek self-direction toward spiritual awareness.

ARIES 7

Birthdays: March 26th-28th

Numerology: 7

Sabian Symbol: A man successfully expressing himself in two realms at once

Marc Edmund Jones Key Word: Proficiency

Jane Ridder-Patrick Healing Body Point: Ears

Crystal Element: Ametrine

Expression: A natural crystal containing amethyst and citrine. Ametrine promotes meditation, boosting psychic abilities and relieving tension; enhances natural talents.

Message: Transmutation of successful ideas and actions through space and time.

Sun Focus: You positively influence change through light and love in the physical and spiritual realms.

Affirmation: I have an aptitude for understanding and enhanced insight.

ARIES 8

Birthdays: March 27th-29th

Numerology: 8

Sabian Symbol: A woman's hat with streamers blown by the east wind.

Marc Edmund Jones Key Word: Excitation

Jane Ridder-Patrick Healing Body Point: Cheekbone

Crystal Element: Banded Agate

Expression: Banded Agate is striped agate; colours can range through the spectrum. Banded Agate promotes communication with astral realms, and supports ingenuity and clear thinking.

Message: Unique, exciting, uplifting experiences.

Sun Focus: You promote uniqueness by respecting positive thought energy that flows toward a purposeful goal.

Affirmation: I am free thinking, with expansive intuition.

ARIES 9
Birthdays: March 28th-30th

Numerology: 9
Sabian Symbol: A crystal gazer
Marc Edmund Jones Key Word: Acuteness
Jane Ridder-Patrick Healing Body Point: Lens of the eyes
Crystal Element: Clear Quartz Crystal
Expression: Clear Quartz is a common mineral. Quartz is very potent, and holds many properties including the concentrating of insight, intuition, healing and divination.
Message: Crystal balls see into the past, define the present, and predict the future.
Sun Focus: Clearly a spiritually gifted person, you focus potentials into reality.
Affirmation: I work responsibly and have profound visions.

ARIES 10
Birthdays: March 29th-31st

Numerology: 10
Sabian Symbol: A man teaching new forms for old symbols
Marc Edmund Jones Key Word: Interpretation
Jane Ridder-Patrick Healing Body Point: Eyeball
Crystal Element: Fossils
Expression: Fossils are the impressions of ancient animals, plants and algae. Fossils aid in the interpretation of developing physical and spiritual life on earth, motivating excellence.
Message: Natural designs tempting us to interpret shape and meaning.
Sun Focus: You understand and explain the significance of karmic and mundane life patterns.
Affirmation: I utilise my skills of interpretation, investigation and communication.

ARIES 11

Birthdays: March 30th–April 1st

Numerology: 11
Sabian Symbol: The president of the country
Marc Edmund Jones Key Word: Idealization
Jane Ridder-Patrick Healing Body Point: Optic nerve
Crystal Element: Green Aventurine
Expression: Green Aventurine is quartz that contains fuchsite mica. Green Aventurine stimulates mental alertness and clarity, with the evolution of ideas bringing career success.
Message: Achieve greatness with the support of many great people.
Sun Focus: Through strength and good fortune you achieve greatness, even under challenging circumstances.
Affirmation: I value and respect others and acknowledge mutual support.

ARIES 12

Birthdays: March 31st–April 2nd

Numerology: 12
Sabian Symbol: A flock of wild geese
Marc Edmund Jones Key Word: Insouciance
Jane Ridder-Patrick Healing Body Point: Tongue
Crystal Element: Barite
Expression: A white mineral, Barite naturally occurs with anglesite and celestite. Utilised by Native Americans in shape-shifting rituals, Barite has Angelic energy.
Message: Negate harsh re-actions; enhance hope and direction.
Sun Focus: You energise life through your spontaneous good nature; use your wings to gain a fresh perspective.
Affirmation: I remain light-hearted in all situations due to my higher awareness.

ARIES 13

Birthdays: March 1st–April 3rd

Numerology: 13

Sabian Symbol: A bomb fails to explode

Marc Edmund Jones Key Word: Impetuousness

Jane Ridder-Patrick Healing Body Point: Ventricles of brain

Crystal Element: Sodalite

Expression: Sodalite is a sodium-bearing mineral. Sodalite fluoresces, energising into the ultraviolet spectrum. Sodalite absolves old patterns, guilt and fear, motivating peaceful change.

Message: Clearing, expanding energy used to auspiciously change your fortune.

Sun Focus: You offer others and yourself a healing way to release and change outdated patterns.

Affirmation: I choose to illuminate and modify my current circumstances.

ARIES 14

Birthdays: April 2nd–4th

Numerology: 14

Sabian Symbol: A serpent coiling near a man and a woman

Marc Edmund Jones Key Word: Revelation

Jane Ridder-Patrick Healing Body Point: Frontal lobes of brain

Crystal Element: Serpentinite

Expression: Serpentinite is a green metamorphic rock. Serpentinite promotes intimate love, attracts money, and develops psychic ability. Snake Totem energy, Kundalini energy.

Message: Shed outdated facades; reveal the bare essentials; promote self-renewal.

Sun Focus: You re-crystallise yourself through passionate interactions with others.

Affirmation: I can transform into an ultimate state of being.

ARIES 15

Birthdays: April 3rd-5th

Numerology: 15
Sabian Symbol: A wise old Indian woman weaves a blanket
Marc Edmund Jones Key Word: Diligence
Jane Ridder-Patrick Healing Body Point: Lateral lobes of brain
Crystal Element: Agatised or Silicified Dinosaur Bone
Expression: Agatised dinosaur bones are fossilised by silica. Ancient dinosaur fossils tie us energetically to the past and aid in past-life memory work, acting as a calming agent.
Message: Concentration, application, visual rewards, spiritual communion.
Sun Focus: You bring into existence practical gifts; you work with other people fulfilling a divine purpose.
Affirmation: I create an outlet for my highest potential.

ARIES 16

Birthdays: April 4th-6th

Numerology: 16
Sabian Symbol: Brownies dancing in the setting sunlight
Marc Edmund Jones Key Word: Invigoration
Jane Ridder-Patrick Healing Body Point: Pons
Crystal Element: Boulder Opal
Expression: Boulder Opal is a colourful opal with a natural backing of ironstone. Boulder Opal promotes a free spirit, amplifies spontaneity and mirrors feelings. Fairy energy abounds.
Message: Festive colour, spirit and energy.
Sun Focus: You inspire others to fly and dance toward freedom and happiness when you embrace your own vitality.
Affirmation: I trip the light fantastic.

ARIES 17

Birthdays: April 5th–7th

Numerology: 17

Sabian Symbol: Two prim spinsters

Marc Edmund Jones Key Word: Divorcement

Jane Ridder-Patrick Healing Body Point: Vertebral canal

Crystal Element: Halite

Expression: Halite or sodium chloride is rock sea salt, and is colourless-to-white, pale blue, or pink. Energetically, Halite, pink in particular, teaches us about love; an alchemical element.

Message: Evaporate blocked feelings; expose truths; purify intentions.

Sun Focus: You are valued for the practical support you offer people and groups.

Affirmation: I am the salt of the earth and a light in the world.

ARIES 18

Birthdays: April 6th–8th

Numerology: 18

Sabian Symbol: An empty hammock

Marc Edmund Jones Key Word: Rumination

Jane Ridder-Patrick Healing Body Point: Nerve connections – synapses

Crystal Element: Cape Amethyst

Expression: Cape Amethyst is a pale purple variety of amethyst originating from Africa. Cape Amethyst is a natural facilitator of rest and contemplation, promoting peacefulness.

Message: Creating space and time invites freedom of thought.

Sun Focus: Contemplation, consideration and meditation advance personal enlightenment.

Affirmation: I use meditation to guide spirit to the centre of my being.

ARIES 19

Birthdays: April 7th-9th

Numerology: 19

Sabian Symbol: A magic carpet ride

Marc Edmund Jones Key Word: Panorama

Jane Ridder-Patrick Healing Body Point: Corpus callosum cerebri

Crystal Element: Black Tektite

Expression: Tektites are glassy, terrestrial rocks formed by impacts from extra-terrestrial objects. Tektites are used as talismans, assisting energy fields, communications, and flying.

Message: Transports spirit and emotion to new heights with ease.

Sun Focus: Rapid transitions between various physical and spiritual states impact your world in magical ways.

Affirmation: I see surrounding influences that others cannot envisage.

ARIES 20

Birthdays: April 8th-10th

Numerology: 20

Sabian Symbol: A young girl feeding birds in winter

Marc Edmund Jones Key Word: Hospitality

Jane Ridder-Patrick Healing Body Point: Hyoid bone

Crystal Element: Rhodochrosite

Expression: Rhodochrosite is a pinkish red, manganese carbonate mineral. Rhodochrosite supports the understanding that we are always loved; it promotes a welcoming energy.

Message: Angelic energy generously satisfies physical and spiritual hunger.

Sun Focus: Your serene nature beautifully comforts your friends and family; you are rewarded with happiness.

Affirmation: I am kind and generous. I provide a safe haven for those in need.

ARIES 21

Birthdays: April 9th-11th

Numerology: 21

Sabian Symbol: A pugilist entering the ring

Marc Edmund Jones Key Word: Exertion

Jane Ridder-Patrick Healing Body Point: Eye muscles

Crystal Element: Hematite

Expression: Hematite is a blackish, silver-grey, iron mineral. Hematite strengthens the mind, is grounding, and helps balance and fortify the body-mind-spirit connection.

Message: Steely determination, iron resolve, defend what it is you believe.

Sun Focus: You face life with great confidence; you empower others with your drive and focus.

Affirmation: I exercise mind, body and spirit – a soul's crusade.

ARIES 22

Birthdays: April 10th-12th

Numerology: 22

Sabian Symbol: The gate to the garden of desire

Marc Edmund Jones Key Word: Prospect

Jane Ridder-Patrick Healing Body Point: Cheek muscles

Crystal Element: Faceted Diamond

Expression: Crystallised carbon, the diamond is the hardest natural crystal. Diamonds amplify pure love and promote purity, beauty, wealth, evolution, and invincibility.

Message: Amplified intentions, refracting inner dreams outward to ideas and action.

Sun Focus: Searching for the beauty in all things promotes brilliant success.

Affirmation: I reflect eternal possibilities in all I do.

ARIES 23

Birthdays: April 11th-13th

Numerology: 23

Sabian Symbol: A woman in pastel colours carrying a heavy and valuable but veiled load.

Marc Edmund Jones Key Word: Reticence

Jane Ridder-Patrick Healing Body Point: Muscles of mastication

Crystal Element: Green Hiddenite

Expression: Hiddenite, the green variety of spodumene, is a valuable gemstone. Hiddenite attracts prosperity, supports emotions, and builds trust. Echoes the High Priestess tarot card.

Message: Access the archaic records and secret universal knowledge.

Sun Focus: You have the ability to anticipate, and prepare people for life's challenges.

Affirmation: I wait in humble anticipation for future endeavours to come to fruition.

ARIES 24

Birthdays: April 12th-14th

Numerology: 24

Sabian Symbol: An open window and a net curtain blowing into a cornucopia

Marc Edmund Jones Key Word: Munificence

Jane Ridder-Patrick Healing Body Point: Zygomatic muscle

Crystal Element: Alexandrite

Expression: Alexandrite is a gemstone variety of chrysoberyl. Alexandrite promotes good luck, spiritual and material prosperity, and abundance.

Message: Bountiful information providing ideas, warnings, details, and inspiration.

Sun Focus: Others wonder at your open, generous spirit; you are a beautiful soul.

Affirmation: I am open to opportunities and I provide opportunities for others.

ARIES 25

Birthdays: April 13th-15th

Numerology: 25

Sabian Symbol: A double promise is revealing

Marc Edmund Jones Key Word: Sensibility

Jane Ridder-Patrick Healing Body Point: Sternocleidomas-
toid muscle

Crystal Element: Banded Iron Stone

Expression: Banded Iron Stone is an ancient, sedimentary, iron oxide and chert rock. Banded Iron Stone promotes transformation, and answers questions from the beginning of time.

Message: Foresight promotes spiritual understanding; cooperation advances social harmony.

Sun Focus: Internal strength and hope pave the way for a confident life; let people see the real you, for you are a visionary.

Affirmation: My empathy resolves fear.

ARIES 26

Birthdays: April 14th-16th

Numerology: 26

Sabian Symbol: A man possessed of more gifts than he can hold

Marc Edmund Jones Key Word: Equipment

Jane Ridder-Patrick Healing Body Point: Skull

Crystal Element: Elbaite

Expression: Elbaite is a colourful gemstone variety of tourmaline. Tourmaline supports spiritual development, protection, grounding, and enhances native talents.

Message: Natural endowment. Harness and develop talents.

Sun Focus: Contributing to life in many ways, you are an instrument that facilitates social advancement.

Affirmation: I realise abundance in my life.

ARIES 27

Birthdays: April 15th-17th

Numerology: 27

Sabian Symbol: Lost opportunity regained through imagination

Marc Edmund Jones Key Word: Reformulation

Jane Ridder-Patrick Healing Body Point: Fornix/frontal bone

Crystal Element: Red Garnet (Pyrope)

Expression: Red Garnet is a hard, glassy gemstone. Red Garnet brings positive thoughts to relationships; it is an excellent stone for manifesting favourable possibilities.

Message: Successful encounters and new ideas through thought and vision.

Sun Focus: Assessment and critical analysis expand your vision, and in turn manifest opportunities.

Affirmation: I am responsible for my self-motivation and the evolution of my ideas.

ARIES 28

Birthdays: April 16th-18th

Numerology: 28

Sabian Symbol: A large disappointed audience

Marc Edmund Jones Key Word: Disjunction

Jane Ridder-Patrick Healing Body Point: Fornix/parietal and occipital bones

Crystal Element: Sard

Expression: Sard is a reddish-brown variety of chalcedony. Traditionally Sard protects from disappointment by softening expectations and stimulating situational awareness.

Message: Expectations are high, but alternatives exist; reconnect to the divine for support.

Sun Focus: Your gift is to unite people in a common purpose, changing the old for improved patterns.

Affirmation: I can realign my internal dialogue and benefit everyone.

ARIES 29

Birthdays: April 17th-19th

Numerology: 29

Sabian Symbol: An angelic choir singing

Marc Edmund Jones Key Word: Veneration

Jane Ridder-Patrick Healing Body Point: Auditory canal

Crystal Element: Celestite

Expression: Celestite is a strontium-sulphate mineral. Celestite connects to the heavenly realms and promotes higher consciousness pursuits. It strengthens clear and honest communication.

Message: Celestial clarity in perceiving angels, listening to divine messages.

Sun Focus: You perceive angels, listen for their harmony in your life, and share your experiences with others.

Affirmation: I join in Angelic adoration, bearing witness to divine love.

ARIES 30

Birthdays: April 18th-20th

Numerology: 30

Sabian Symbol: A pond, a duck and ducklings.

Marc Edmund Jones Key Word: Reliability

Jane Ridder-Patrick Healing Body Point: Parotid gland

Crystal Element: Rhyolite (Rainforest Jasper)

Expression: Rhyolite is an extrusive volcanic rock that appears in a variety of colours and textures. Rhyolite promotes happy people entering your life, particularly children.

Message: Safe, secure and happy home environment.

Sun Focus: You are dependable and faithful, helping those around you with grace and love.

Affirmation: I am worthy of trust; people look to me for guidance.

TAURUS 1

Birthdays: April 19th-20th

Numerology: 31

Sabian Symbol: A clear mountain stream

Marc Edmund Jones Key Word: Resourcefulness

Jane Ridder-Patrick Healing Body Point: Throat, gullet

Crystal Element: Clear Spinel

Expression: Clear Spinel is a magnesium, aluminium oxide gemstone. Clear
Spinel rejuvenates mind, body and spirit, promoting new avenues for success.

Message: Unique, individual messages through simple channels.

Sun Focus: Your fresh inspiration and free spirit flow towards others, promoting
flexibility and rejuvenation.

Affirmation: I live naturally in all ways.

TAURUS 2

Birthdays: April 20th -21st

Numerology: 32

Sabian Symbol: An electrical storm

Marc Edmund Jones Key Word: Transformation

Jane Ridder-Patrick Healing Body Point: Palate

Crystal Element: Electrum or Fulgurite

Expression: Electrum is a naturally occurring, gold-silver-copper metal.
Fulgurite is lightning-fused quartz. Spiritually, both crystal elements aid in
transition; echoes the Tower tarot card.

Message: Alchemy, power and force transform mundane life to that of purest
gold.

Sun Focus: Sudden and unexpected life events act as a catalyst for awareness,
insight, and purification.

Affirmation: My talent for transformation brings immediate revelations.

TAURUS 3

Birthdays: April 21st-23rd

Numerology: 33

Sabian Symbol: Steps up to a lawn blooming with clover

Marc Edmund Jones Key Word: Hopefulness

Jane Ridder-Patrick Healing Body Point: Pharynx

Crystal Element: Moss Agate

Expression: A white variety of agate, Moss Agate has green manganese and iron oxide dendritic inclusions. Moss Agate traditionally promotes abundance, good health, and prosperity.

Message: Hope, inspiration, kindness, a smooth life journey.

Sun Focus: Your optimism throughout life successfully promotes personal and collective growth and love.

Affirmation: My mature intentions nurture understanding.

TAURUS 4

Birthday: April 23rd - 24th

Numerology: 34

Sabian Symbol: The rainbow's pot of gold

Marc Edmund Jones Key Word: Faith

Jane Ridder-Patrick Healing Body Point: Uvula

Crystal Element: Goldstone

Expression: A man-made stone made of glass and copper glitter. Alchemically symbolising the transmutation of gold process, Goldstone is uplifting, energising, and increases happiness.

Message: Sustain spiritual pursuits; discover treasures of the human realm.

Sun Focus: You are a confident person. Trust in the divine; show others how to remain virtuous.

Affirmation: I have faith, hope and love.

TAURUS 5

Birthdays: April 24th-26th

Numerology: 35

Sabian Symbol: A widow at an open grave

Marc Edmund Jones Key Word: Reorientation

Jane Ridder-Patrick Healing Body Point: Pharyngeal cavity

Crystal Element: Geode

Expression: Geodes have a crystalline cavity filled with quartz, amethyst, agate, jasper. Offering protection, cooperation, purification and harmony, Geodes specifically guide the spirit upward.

Message: Elevated awareness of self with regard to time and place.

Sun Focus: Personal relationships have substance beyond material existence; share your belief systems with others.

Affirmation: I sense beyond the physical, and believe.

TAURUS 6

Birthdays: April 25th-27th

Numerology: 36

Sabian Symbol: A bridge being built across a gorge

Marc Edmund Jones Key Word: Channelship

Jane Ridder-Patrick Healing Body Point: Larynx

Crystal Element: Astrophyllite

Expression: Astrophyllite is a golden-yellow, titanium mineral. Astrophyllite reconnects the inner and outer realms, between self and others, the divine and the mundane.

Message: Positive transitions, supportive when moving on to a new evolutionary stage.

Sun Focus: Not limited by space and time, your insight, intuition and foresight connect people to places and circumstances.

Affirmation: I have a safe pathway through life.

TAURUS 7

Birthdays: April 26th-28th

Numerology: 37

Sabian Symbol: A woman of Samaria

Marc Edmund Jones Key Word: Awakening

Jane Ridder-Patrick Healing Body Point: Vocal cords

Crystal Element: Soapstone

Expression: Soapstone is a metamorphic rock. Soapstone has hidden power and strength; it retains and transmits heat, and is physically and spiritually warming. Goddess Energy.

Message: Understated kind service, love, and honour; life is revitalised.

Sun Focus: Through your kindness, you draw attention to causes that lead to the betterment of society.

Affirmation: My comforting deeds soothe the spirit.

TAURUS 8

Birthdays: April 27th-29th

Numerology: 38

Sabian Symbol: A sleigh without snow

Marc Edmund Jones Key Word: Sustainment

Jane Ridder-Patrick Healing Body Point: Cervical nerves

Crystal Element: Larvikite

Expression: Larvikite is a coarse-grained, feldspar-rich rock with blue flash reflections. Spiritually, Larvikite promotes durability, steadiness and strength, turning dreams into reality.

Message: To everything there is a season, a time to every purpose under heaven.

Sun Focus: You are a vehicle for environmental concerns; your support through practical actions makes you a mover and a shaker.

Affirmation: By maintaining my purpose I support others in their divine purpose.

TAURUS 9

Birthdays: April 28th–30th

Numerology: 39

Sabian Symbol: A decorated Christmas tree

Marc Edmund Jones Key Word: Symbolization

Jane Ridder-Patrick Healing Body Point: Jugular veins

Crystal Element: Fuchsite

Expression: Fuchsite is chromium-rich, green mica. Spiritually, fuchsite channels physical and emotional healing; it invites friendliness, compassion and lightheartedness into the home.

Message: Goodwill, loving intentions, respect for all celebrations of spirit.

Sun Focus: Your strengths are: promoting hope, uniting people with mutual ideals, sharing joyful experiences.

Affirmation: I create harmony using meaningful signs and ceremonial actions.

TAURUS 10

Birthdays: April 29th–May 1st

Numerology: 40

Sabian Symbol: A Red Cross nurse

Marc Edmund Jones Key Word: Enlistment

Jane Ridder-Patrick Healing Body Point: Cervical veins

Crystal Element: Red Calcite

Expression: Iron-stained calcium carbonate is termed Red Calcite. Red Calcite fortifies courage and strength, reduces physical stress, and increases energy to handle survival situations.

Message: Call attention to caring and allow yourself to be cared for.

Sun Focus: While caring for others, travel, adventure and discipline complete your life.

Affirmation: My skill is in immediate action; I save lives.

TAURUS 11

Birthdays: April 30th–May 2nd

Numerology: 41
Sabian Symbol: A woman sprinkling flowers
Marc Edmund Jones Key Word: Care
Jane Ridder-Patrick Healing Body Point: Cervical and
  brachial plexi
Crystal Element: Rhodonite
Expression: Rhodonite is a red, manganese-rich pyroxene mineral. Traditionally
  Rhodonite boosts self esteem, compassion, beauty and kindness, encouraging
  gentleness and self care.
Message: Gentle, kind growth of intentions manifesting into reality.
Sun Focus: Honesty and kindness, expressed through genuine forethought,
  gather true friends and abundant blessings.
Affirmation: I am involved in fruitful relationships.

TAURUS 12

Birthdays: May 1st–3rd

Numerology: 42
Sabian Symbol: Window-shoppers
Marc Edmund Jones Key Word: Visualization
Jane Ridder-Patrick Healing Body Point: Cervical and
  brachial plexi
Crystal Element: Window Quartz Crystal
Expression: Window Quartz Crystals have a rhombic facet below the apex.
  Window Quartz Crystals enhance the qualities of any stones positioned close
  by, and act as energy amplifiers.
Message: Looking, seeing, appraising, making realistic assessments.
Sun Focus: Others respect your evaluations as you see with openness and clarity;
  you provide accurate information and responses.
Affirmation: I use visual cues to make valuable comparisons and judgements.

TAURUS 13

Birthdays: May 2nd-4th

Numerology: 43

Sabian Symbol: A man handling baggage

Marc Edmund Jones Key Word: Industry

Jane Ridder-Patrick Healing Body Point: Cervical and brachial plexi

Crystal Element: Bauxite

Expression: Bauxite is an orangey-brown, aluminium-rich, sedimentary rock. Bauxite absorbs negativity and clarifies native talents; an alchemical element fostering reformation of spirit.

Message: Take control of the situation and deliver positive outcomes.

Sun Focus: Application and diligence afford you supportive environments to move forward and prosper.

Affirmation: I am flexible and resilient.

TAURUS 14

Birthdays: May 3rd-5th

Numerology: 44

Sabian Symbol: Shellfish groping and children playing

Marc Edmund Jones Key Word: Emergence

Jane Ridder-Patrick Healing Body Point: True vocal cords

Crystal Element: Mother of Pearl

Expression: Known as Nacre, Mother of Pearl is a naturally-occurring, iridescent, calcium carbonate. Mother of Pearl intensifies intuition and creativity. It is highly protective for children.

Message: Child-like innocence, simplicity, joy and carefree play.

Sun Focus: Your charm shines happiness and fun into people's hearts and their daily activities.

Affirmation: I live in harmony with all that is around me.

TAURUS 15

Birthdays: May 4th-6th

Numerology: 45

Sabian Symbol: A man wearing a muffler and a stylish silk hat

Marc Edmund Jones Key Word: Sophistication

Jane Ridder-Patrick Healing Body Point: Epiglottis

Crystal Element: Wulfenite

Expression: Wulfenite is a crystalline, molybdenum and lead ore mineral. Wulfenite is a warming crystal, invigorating emotions and motivating action.

Message: Carefree elegance in movement and manner, admired by peers.

Sun Focus: You have a conspicuously unique style, a trendsetter in all you do.

Affirmation: My stylish individuality adds to my visual appeal.

TAURUS 16

Birthdays: May 5th-7th

Numerology: 46

Sabian Symbol: An old man attempting vainly to reveal the mysteries

Marc Edmund Jones Key Word: Pertinacity

Jane Ridder-Patrick Healing Body Point: Carotid arteries

Crystal Element: Clay (Kaolinite)

Expression: Clay is fine-grained particles including kaolinite. Clay captures and stores emotions and information, and enhances accurate and detailed work.

Message: Compassion and respect, striving together to reach enlightenment.

Sun Focus: Through your persistence and determination you attract divine blessings; record them for future reference.

Affirmation: I will keep preserving with compassion and grace.

TAURUS 17

Birthdays: May 6th- 8th

Numerology: 47

Sabian Symbol: A symbolic battle between swords and torches

Marc Edmund Jones Key Word: Resolution

Jane Ridder-Patrick Healing Body Point: Thyroid gland and tonsils

Crystal Element: Jacinth

Expression: Jacinth is a red variety of zircon. Jacinth is a stone of deep wisdom and helps promises and sacred vows to remain intact, in line with our highest intention.

Message: Richness in spirit, a sense of justice, guided by strong convictions.

Sun Focus: Single-mindedness and self-determination motivate you to answer important questions.

Affirmation: I am balanced, thoughtful, and energetic.

TAURUS 18

Birthdays: May 7th-9th

Numerology: 48

Sabian Symbol: A woman holding a bag out of a window

Marc Edmund Jones Key Word: Facilitation

Jane Ridder-Patrick Healing Body Point: Lymph vessels

Crystal Element: Anthophyllite

Expression: Anthophyllite is a distinctive, brown-coloured amphibole mineral. Anthophyllite serves to purify and cleanse the body, mind and spirit.

Message: Movement of ideas, karma and feelings. Light and space are invited in.

Sun Focus: Your personal magnetism facilitates cooperation and achievement.

Affirmation: I surrender my limitations to accomplish greatness.

TAURUS 19

Birthdays: May 8th-10th

Numerology: 49

Sabian Symbol: A newly formed continent rising majestically from the ocean

Marc Edmund Jones Key Word: Originality

Jane Ridder-Patrick Healing Body Point: Maxillary artery

Crystal Element: Olivine

Expression: Olivine is an olive-green mineral, a fundamental component of the earth's mantle. Olivine is a healing mineral, facilitating awareness and access to the earth's energy grid.

Message: Powerfully promotes new opportunities and growth through raw energy.

Sun Focus: Growth through powerful decision-making positively affects those around you.

Affirmation: Newfound lands and spirit provide me with every opportunity to succeed.

TAURUS 20

Birthdays: May 9th-11th

Numerology: 50

Sabian Symbol: Wisps of cloud streaming across the sky

Marc Edmund Jones Key Word: Exaltation

Jane Ridder-Patrick Healing Body Point: Occiput

Crystal Element: Spotted Lapis

Expression: Spotted Lapis is Lapis Lazuli rich in calcite. Spotted Lapis promotes love and respect, lightens emotions, and allows stress, worries, fear and anger to drift away.

Message: Anticipating change in life force, energy, and vigour.

Sun Focus: Your virtuous thoughts and prayers really do make a difference in life.

Affirmation: I see evidence of fleeting realities that guide me to greater spiritual heights.

TAURUS 21

Birthdays: May 10th-12th

Numerology: 51
Sabian Symbol: A finger pointing in an open book
Marc Edmund Jones Key Word: Confirmation
Jane Ridder-Patrick Healing Body Point: Arteries of nasal cavities
Crystal Element: Slate
Expression: Slate is a fine-grained, metamorphic rock that splits into thin sheets. Spiritually, slate enhances memory work, accurate history, and record keeping.
Message: Blank slates to create on, translate and understand, then wipe clean.
Sun Focus: Your systematic investigation skills help you establish facts, and compile them for future reference.
Affirmation: I confirm my life direction by examining the facts.

TAURUS 22

Birthdays: May 11th-13th

Numerology: 52
Sabian Symbol: White dove over troubled waters
Marc Edmund Jones Key Word: Guidance
Jane Ridder-Patrick Healing Body Point: Tongue muscles
Crystal Element: Dioptase
Expression: Dioptase is a rare, copper mineral. Dioptase brings profound happiness, heals past hurts on all levels, and empowers the heart to be guided into a place of strength and confidence.
Message: Desire goodness, with peaceful confidence.
Sun Focus: You provide messages of hope and confidence, with graceful serenity.
Affirmation: I hold a true course and direct others to safety.

TAURUS 23

Birthdays: May 12th-14th

Numerology: 53
Sabian Symbol: A jewellery shop
Marc Edmund Jones Key Word: Preservation
Jane Ridder-Patrick Healing Body Point: Teeth
Crystal Element: Emerald
Expression: Emerald is gemstone-quality, green beryl. Emeralds have an extensive list of spiritual attributes including protection, spiritual growth, faith, and intelligent communication.
Message: Incorporating protection, betterment, sensation and radiance.
Sun Focus: Precious soul, you have many treasures – spiritual, emotional, creative, to name a few.
Affirmation: I protect the best values in life.

TAURUS 24

Birthdays: May 13th-15th

Numerology: 54
Sabian Symbol: An Indian with his speeding horse, and a scalp hanging from his belt.
Marc Edmund Jones Key Word: Command
Jane Ridder-Patrick Healing Body Point: Upper jaw
Crystal Element: Red Jasper
Expression: Jasper is a variety of quartz. Jasper is an excellent grounding stone, generous in providing courage and personal independence.
Message: Loyalty, strength, justice, admiration and respect.
Sun Focus: Ferocity, skill, balance and coordination aid you in standing up for human rights.
Affirmation: I rely on my own determination, focus and energy to move me toward success.

TAURUS 25

Birthdays: May 14th-16th

Numerology: 55
Sabian Symbol: A large and well-kept public park
Marc Edmund Jones Key Word: Recreation
Jane Ridder-Patrick Healing Body Point: Lower jaw
Crystal Element: Brazilianite
Expression: Brazilianite is an unusual, green-yellow, phosphate-based gemstone. This stone promotes friendship, lightens auras, and helps heal minor ailments.
Message: Refresh and renew, enjoy and relax.
Sun Focus: Your playful, comfortable nature facilitates for many people an escape from the mundane activities in life.
Affirmation: I am completely refreshed after communing with nature.

TAURUS 26

Birthdays: May 15th-17th

Numerology: 56
Sabian Symbol: A Spaniard serenading his señorita
Marc Edmund Jones Key Word: Constancy
Jane Ridder-Patrick Healing Body Point: Nasal bone
Crystal Element: Rubellite
Expression: Rubellite, a natural tourmaline, sparkles through the red, pink and purple colour range. Traditionally Rubellite strengthens love, passion, emotional balance, and devotion.
Message: Overflowing passion, devotion sustained by harmony.
Sun Focus: Extravagance, beauty and love permeate your life; you let everyone see your passion for living.
Affirmation: I show love through care, attention, and clear intention.

TAURUS 27

Birthdays: May 16th-18th

Numerology: 57
Sabian Symbol: An Indian squaw selling beads
Marc Edmund Jones Key Word: Detachment
Jane Ridder-Patrick Healing Body Point: Atlas
Crystal Element: Turquoise
Expression: Turquoise is a valuable stone. Prized equally by many cultures, turquoise is a protective stone, aiding in truthful communication and meditation.
Message: Persuasive influences, alternative courses for unconditional love.
Sun Focus: Wisdom and secrecy are your strengths; others offer you goodwill.
Affirmation: I accept, release, and allow space for the exchange of energy.

TAURUS 28

Birthdays: May 17th-18th

Numerology: 58
Sabian Symbol: A woman pursued by mature romance
Marc Edmund Jones Key Word: Persuasion
Jane Ridder-Patrick Healing Body Point: Deltoid muscle
Crystal Element: Morganite
Expression: Morganite is pink, gem-quality beryl. Morganite inspires devotion, compassion, equality, empathy and patience, motivating a more mature loving life.
Message: Aroused by the soft, gentle exploration of love, with sensitive boundaries.
Sun Focus: You appear completed through your consideration and perfected sensibilities.
Affirmation: My intuitive awareness sustains beautiful sentiment.

TAURUS 29

Birthdays: May 18th-19th

Numerology: 59
Sabian Symbol: Two cobblers working at a table
Marc Edmund Jones Key Word: Capability
Jane Ridder-Patrick Healing Body Point: Main neck
   muscles
Crystal Element: Gabbro
Expression: Gabbro is a dark-coloured plutonic rock, composed of plagioclase
   and pyroxene. Gabbro spiritually balances and enhances personal magnetism
   and cooperation at work.
Message: Practical relationships manufacture opportunities to fulfil spiritual
   obligations.
Sun Focus: Your specific skill set forms the basis for support and reward.
Affirmation: I utilise my tools, skills and passion to fulfil my vocation.

TAURUS 30

Birthdays: May 19th-20th

Numerology: 60
Sabian Symbol: A peacock parading on an ancient lawn
Marc Edmund Jones Key Word: Aloofness
Jane Ridder-Patrick Healing Body Point: Trapezius muscle
Crystal Element: Peacock Ore (Bornite)
Expression: Peacock Ore tarnishes to brilliant iridescent blue, green, and
   purple. Peacock Ore clears the mind, aids in concentration, and promotes
   beauty through self-confidence.
Message: Success and confidence displayed, avail yourself of every advantage.
Sun Focus: Reserved contentment and prestige, derived from radiating
   self-assuredness.
Affirmation: I enjoy grandeur, mystery, spectacle and fanfare.

GEMINI 1
Birthdays: May 21st–22nd

Numerology: 61
Sabian Symbol: A glass-bottomed boat reveals undersea wonders
Marc Edmund Jones Key Word: Curiosity
Jane Ridder-Patrick Healing Body Point: Trachea
Crystal Element: Petoskey Stone
Expression: Petoskey Stone is an ancient fossilized coral. Spiritually, Petoskey amplifies Neptune's energy, unlocking the emotional self.
Message: An Atlantean shift in energy, glimpses of deep unconscious thought.
Sun Focus: Your phenomenal capacity for friendship brings to life: community well-being, admiration, and respect.
Affirmation: Natural diversity inspires wonder and awe in me.

GEMINI 2
Birthdays: May 22nd–23rd

Numerology: 62
Sabian Symbol: Santa Claus furtively filling stockings
Marc Edmund Jones Key Word: Prodigality
Jane Ridder-Patrick Healing Body Point: Oesophagus
Crystal Element: Red Agate
Expression: Agate is a widely used term applied to banded silica; iron oxide creates Red Agate. Red Agate is a high-energy stone, increasing self-confidence and harmony within groups.
Message: Generous spirit, the bringer of goodwill, especially toward children.
Sun Focus: You provide hope in difficult times; you remind others how to wish and dream and why these emotions are important.
Affirmation: I look forward to surprise gifts and the emotions they awaken in me.

GEMINI 3
Birthdays: May 23rd–24th

Numerology: 63
Sabian Symbol: The garden of the Tuileries
Marc Edmund Jones Key Word: Luxury
Jane Ridder-Patrick Healing Body Point: Upper right
   pulmonary lobe
Crystal Element: Orthoclase
Expression: Orthoclase is an important igneous mineral. Orthoclase brings a
   sense of refinement and appreciation of the finer things in life.
Message: Noble and worthy traits are idealised and replicated.
Sun Focus: You are a guide, showing others the way to a comfortable and
   tranquil life.
Affirmation: I look forward to a time for indulgence and pleasure in my life.

GEMINI 4
Birthdays: May 24th–25th

Numerology: 64
Sabian Symbol: Holly and mistletoe
Marc Edmund Jones Key Word: Ritualization
Jane Ridder-Patrick Healing Body Point: Lower right
   pulmonary lobe
Crystal Element: Watermelon Tourmaline
Expression: Watermelon Tourmaline has a pink-red core and green edges.
   Watermelon Tourmaline promotes love, protection, and family acceptance.
Message: Joyful ceremonies bring together family and community.
Sun Focus: Your ability to organise celebrations of the spirit promotes a return
   to simple delights with family and friends.
Affirmation: I feel peace and joy as I feel safe.

GEMINI 5

Birthdays: May 25th-26th

Numerology: 65

Sabian Symbol: A radical magazine

Marc Edmund Jones Key Word: Tangency

Jane Ridder-Patrick Healing Body Point: Upper left pulmonary lobe

Crystal Element: Crazy Lace Agate

Expression: Crazy Lace Agate is brightly coloured, elaborately banded silica rock. Crazy Lace Agate elevates the mind, promotes eloquence in communication, and buoys self-confidence.

Message: Clear and honest communication; sensational and contrasting points of view.

Sun Focus: Courage, determination and self-promotion open the way for new endeavours.

Affirmation: I investigate modern culture through information exchange.

GEMINI 6

Birthday: May 26th-28th

Numerology: 66

Sabian Symbol: Drilling for oil

Marc Edmund Jones Key Word: Speculation

Jane Ridder-Patrick Healing Body Point: Lower left pulmonary lobe

Crystal Element: Augite

Expression: Augite is a dark green-black, magnesium-rich pyroxene. Spiritually, Augite offers alternative routes for discovering riches, acting as a guide on the path to awareness.

Message: Pinpoint options and evaluate risks, while acquiring knowledge and resources.

Sun Focus: You have the ability to persevere till you succeed; you show others where riches are to be found and that finding them is worth the effort.

Affirmation: I know meaningful exploration unearths unforeseen wealth.

GEMINI 7
Birthdays: May 26th-27th

Numerology: 67
Sabian Symbol: An old-fashioned well
Marc Edmund Jones Key Word: Recompense
Jane Ridder-Patrick Healing Body Point: Apex of lungs
Crystal Element: Limestone

Expression: Pure Limestone is a white sedimentary rock. Many spiritual locations are found in and around Limestone locations. A subtle but strong energy, Limestone acts as a conduit for positive forces.
Message: A natural reverence for purity and spirit.
Sun Focus: You connect deeply with emotion and spirit, accessing this resource to find creative solutions to issues that arise within your life.
Affirmation: I live an enriching, nourishing, healthy life.

GEMINI 8
Birthdays: May 27th-29th

Numerology: 68
Sabian Symbol: An industrial strike
Marc Edmund Jones Key Word: Protest
Jane Ridder-Patrick Healing Body Point: Bronchi
Crystal Element: Smoky Quartz
Expression: Smoky Quartz is quartz that through natural and/or artificial radiation has turned dark in colour. Traditionally used to cope with stress, fear and panic, it is a potent crystal for protection.
Message: Modern safeguards encourage boundary-setting and productivity.
Sun Focus: You are a vehicle for expression, standing up for personal rights and social justices.
Affirmation: I ardently declare my personal truth.

GEMINI 9
Birthdays: May 28th–30th

Numerology: 69
Sabian Symbol: A quiver filled with arrows
Marc Edmund Jones Key Word: Preparation
Jane Ridder-Patrick Healing Body Point: Pulmonary arteries
Crystal Element: Flint
Expression: During the Stone Age, Flint was used for tools; it is a type of quartz. Traditionally, Flint stone resonates with fire and air, energy and thought, and spurs on action.
Message: Strength and accuracy, combined with stability.
Sun Focus: A successful balance between thought and action promotes camaraderie and sportsmanship.
Affirmation: I am poised and confident, ready to skilfully aim my ideas towards action.

GEMINI 10
Birthdays: May 30th–31st

Numerology: 70
Sabian Symbol: An airplane appears to free-fall towards earth
Marc Edmund Jones Key Word: Crisis
Jane Ridder-Patrick Healing Body Point: Hilum of lungs
Crystal Element: Eudialyte
Expression: Eudialyte is a red, orange, or pink cyclosilicate mineral. Spiritually, Eudialyte reflects the pace of modern life and helps calm workplace anxiety.
Message: Recycling energy, refining expectations through new experiences.
Sun Focus: Your constant strength of character supports others to soar through life's ups and downs.
Affirmation: I am prepared to respond quickly to any emergency.

GEMINI 11
Birthdays: May 31st-June 1st

Numerology: 71

Sabian Symbol: Newly opened lands offer the pioneer new opportunities.

Marc Edmund Jones Key Word: Identification

Jane Ridder-Patrick Healing Body Point: Thymus gland

Crystal Element: Tsavorite

Expression: Tsavorite is a green garnet, rich in vanadium and chromium. Traditionally, Tsavorite is a source of illumination for physical and spiritual growth.

Message: A fresh start, new beginnings, nourishing all stages of spiritual evolution.

Sun Focus: You recognise others' pain and empathise with them, providing avenues for growth and understanding.

Affirmation: I see great opportunities born from simplicity.

GEMINI 12
Birthdays: June 1st-3rd

Numerology: 72

Sabian Symbol: A slave girl demands her rights

Marc Edmund Jones Key Word: Growth

Jane Ridder-Patrick Healing Body Point: Tracheal mucosa

Crystal Element: Cubic Zirconia

Expression: Cubic Zirconia is synthesized and optically flawless, primarily used as a diamond simulant. Contemporary in energy, Cubic Zirconia supports a modern lifestyle.

Message: Embracing scattered energies and transforming them into intense rays.

Sun Focus: Passionate communication reforms old patterns, and ensures new patterns emerge and are sustained.

Affirmation: I command attention and establish new standards.

GEMINI 13
Birthdays: June 2nd–4th

Numerology: 73
Sabian Symbol: A great musician at his piano
Marc Edmund Jones Key Word: Achievement
Jane Ridder-Patrick Healing Body Point: Pulmonary veins
Crystal Element: Cinnabar Opal
Expression: Cinnabar Opal contains mercury sulphide that accentuates this red opal. Spiritually, Cinnabar Opal channels universal principles to raise and harmonize the collective consciousness.
Message: Alchemical transmutation, artistic sound, a path for emotional release.
Sun Focus: You have refined communication skills; music in particular provides happiness and comfort to you.
Affirmation: I am grateful for the music in my life; it gives me great joy.

GEMINI 14
Birthdays: June 3rd–5th

Numerology: 74
Sabian Symbol: A conversation by telepathy
Marc Edmund Jones Key Word: Intimation
Jane Ridder-Patrick Healing Body Point: Clavicle
Crystal Element: Tanzanite
Expression: Tanzanite is the popular, blue-purple, gemstone variety of zoisite. Tanzanite accelerates human development spiritually and emotionally by opening human perceptions to the divine.
Message: Intuition and protection; communicating spiritually balancing ideas.
Sun Focus: You manage to conquer space and time limitations with a unique and sensitive communication technique.
Affirmation: The bridge between spirit and consciousness is strong within me.

GEMINI 15
Birthdays: June 4th-6th

Numerology: 75
Sabian Symbol: Two Dutch children talking
Marc Edmund Jones Key Word: Clarification
Jane Ridder-Patrick Healing Body Point: Scapulae
Crystal Element: Aplite (Dalmatian Stone)
Expression: Aplite is fine-grained, silica- and feldspar-rich, speckled, igneous rock. Spiritually, this stone unites like-minded people to achieve distinct goals, and enhances positive educational outcomes.
Message: Candid conversations; expressive play; care for those close to you.
Sun Focus: Through your ingenuousness you help others talk and listen; you find explaining the complexities of life effortless.
Affirmation: I promote the culture of intelligence through peace and awareness.

GEMINI 16
Birthdays: June 5th-7th

Numerology: 76
Sabian Symbol: A woman suffragist haranguing
Marc Edmund Jones Key Word: Indignation
Jane Ridder-Patrick Healing Body Point: Pleura
Crystal Element: Green Calcite
Expression: Calcite is the mineral calcium carbonate; metallic impurities make the calcite green. Green Calcite is best utilised to balance and heal mental and emotional states.
Message: Ground, centre and stabilize to provide a foundation for personal power to emerge.
Sun Focus: You pursue alternative routes to activate change in your life; your determination manifests change.
Affirmation: I motivate myself and others into positive action.

GEMINI 17
Birthdays: June 6th–8th

Numerology: 77
Sabian Symbol: Youthfulness dissolves into a mature thinking
Marc Edmund Jones Key Word: Development
Jane Ridder-Patrick Healing Body Point: First rib
Crystal Element: Banded Amethyst or Chevron Amethyst
Expression: Chevron Amethyst has clear bands of purple amethyst and clear quartz. Banded Amethyst combines quartz and amethyst to promote relaxation, peace and spiritual awareness.
Message: Know your true self; others are reflected in you.
Sun Focus: You realise that the divine is circular, that the purity of childhood is at the same point as spiritual enlightenment.
Affirmation: My ideas evolve to maturity with ease.

GEMINI 18
Birthdays: June 7th–9th

Numerology: 78
Sabian Symbol: Two Chinese men talking Chinese in a western crowd
Marc Edmund Jones Key Word: Difference
Jane Ridder-Patrick Healing Body Point: Second rib
Crystal Element: Green Jade – Jadeite
Expression: Jadeite is one of two types of green pyroxene minerals. Many cultures utilise the power in Jade to promote abundance, good health and prosperity.
Message: Challenging fundamental characteristics, accepting diversity.
Sun Focus: Eccentricity is one of your most prominent attributes; you are unique.
Affirmation: With my friends I form strong karmic bonds.

GEMINI 19
Birthdays: June 8th-10th

Sabian Symbol: A large archaic volume
Marc Edmund Jones Key Word: Background
Numerology: 79
Jane Ridder-Patrick Healing Body Point: Laryngeal muscles
Crystal Element: Lavender Quartz
Expression: Lavender Quartz is a type of quarz with a lilac hue. Lavender Quartz inspires innate clairsentience, clairaudience, and clairvoyance, as well as other communication skills.
Message: Verification of karmic conditions, unlocking universal information.
Sun Focus: You notice what others see and value, and you share this information through various media.
Affirmation: I value recorded information, and the energy contained within it.

GEMINI 20
Birthdays: June 9th-11th

Numerology: 80
Sabian Symbol: A cafeteria
Marc Edmund Jones Key Word: Supply
Jane Ridder-Patrick Healing Body Point: Third rib
Crystal Element: Tin
Expression: Tin is a silvery-white metal utilized since the Bronze Age. A significant alchemical element associated with the operation of dissolution, tin promotes situational awareness.
Message: Contribute provisions; sustenance for everyone.
Sun Focus: A practical person, you provide resources to help others survive physically and spiritually.
Affirmation: I freely provide nourishment for the mind, body and soul.

GEMINI 21

Birthdays: June 10th-12th

Numerology: 81

Sabian Symbol: A labour demonstration

Marc Edmund Jones Key Word: Representation

Jane Ridder-Patrick Healing Body Point: Arm muscles

Crystal Element: Bronzite

Expression: A type of pyroxene, Bronzite is a green-brown mineral. Bronzite interacts with group energy, bolstering group dynamics while confidently supporting individual needs.

Message: Physical declarations trigger reform in human activity.

Sun Focus: You live life with passion and vigour, remaining young at heart, and with idealistic values that *do* change the world.

Affirmation: I am a powerful individual. I support revolutionary action for organisations.

GEMINI 22

Birthdays: June 11th-13th

Numerology: 82

Sabian Symbol: A barn dance

Marc Edmund Jones Key Word: Gregariousness

Jane Ridder-Patrick Healing Body Point: Upper arm

Crystal Element: Clear Apophyllite

Expression: Clear Apophyllite is a group of beautiful phyllosilicate crystals. Metaphysically, Apophyllite clearly connects physical forms to spiritual realms.

Message: Attune your body through movement, rhythm and music.

Sun Focus: You are a sociable person, welcoming time spent in the company of like-minded people.

Affirmation: I support my friendships with cheerful merriment and companionship.

GEMINI 23
Birthdays: June 12th-14th

Numerology: 83
Sabian Symbol: Three fledglings in a nest high in a tree
Marc Edmund Jones Key Word: Elevation
Jane Ridder-Patrick Healing Body Point: Head of the humerus
Crystal Element: Green Quartz (Nickel Quartz)

Expression: Green Quartz is nickel bearing quartzite. Spiritually, Green Quartz promotes physical growth and enhances prayers and personal affirmations.
Message: A secluded haven promoting comfort, safety, and protection.
Sun Focus: You take care of your friends, acting as a sanctuary for those around you.
Affirmation: I support transformation and growth in my world.

GEMINI 24
Birthdays: June 13th-15th

Numerology: 84
Sabian Symbol: Children skating on ice
Marc Edmund Jones Key Word: Fun
Jane Ridder-Patrick Healing Body Point: Olecranon
Crystal Element: Siberian Quartz
Expression: Siberian Quartz is man-made, and is quartz infused with cobalt. A modern crystal, Siberian Quartz puts zing into life; it also promotes open-mindedness and mental clarity.
Message: Encouraging happiness and balance, joyful experiences.
Sun Focus: You are a fun, freedom loving, outdoor adventurer; enjoyable experiences are important to you.
Affirmation: I choose a lifetime of liberating vitality and healthy activity.

GEMINI 25

Birthdays: June 14th-16th

Numerology: 85
Sabian Symbol: A man trimming palms
Marc Edmund Jones Key Word: Enhancement
Jane Ridder-Patrick Healing Body Point: Radius

Crystal Element: Petrified Palm or Fern Wood
Expression: Petrified Palm or Fern belongs to the group of silicified, fossilised woods. Spiritually, this crystal element reveals the prerequisites and boundaries needed in a given situation.
Message: Stability and direction, combined with agility and radiance.
Sun Focus: You are an agreeable person; be confident you have what you need to realise your full potential.
Affirmation: I choose to reach out and beautify my surroundings.

GEMINI 26

Birthdays: June 15th-17th

Numerology: 86
Sabian Symbol: Winter frost in the woods
Marc Edmund Jones Key Word: Splendour
Jane Ridder-Patrick Healing Body Point: Wrist bone
Crystal Element: Snow Quartz
Expression: Snow Quartz is a milky, cloudy variety of quartz rock. Snow Quartz channels freedom, tranquillity and renewal; it offers a pure energy.
Message: Momentary recognition of fresh, clear, brilliant majesty.
Sun Focus: You are a distinguished person who shares attention and praise with others.
Affirmation: I value pristine, natural beauty; it overtakes conscious thought.

GEMINI 27
Birthdays: June 16th–18th

Numerology: 87
Sabian Symbol: A gypsy coming out of the woods
Marc Edmund Jones Key Word: Expenditure
Jane Ridder-Patrick Healing Body Point: Fingers
Crystal Element: Smithsonite

Expression: A zinc carbonate, Smithsonite can be found in a variety of colours. Smithsonite attracts positive opportunities and friends, and supports positive karmic patterns.

Message: Alternative lifestyles, individuality, curious use of talents.

Sun Focus: You may appear as a rebel with a cause. Your investment of time and effort in helping others reflects favourably on you.

Affirmation: By changing perspective, I look forward to future endeavours.

GEMINI 28
Birthdays: June 17th–19th

Numerology: 88
Sabian Symbol: A man declared bankrupt
Marc Edmund Jones Key Word: Deliverance
Jane Ridder-Patrick Healing Body Point: Metacarpal bones
Crystal Element: Nickel

Expression: Nickel is a silvery-white, resistant metal. Nickel promotes a sustained ability to empathize with others, particularly those who need help.

Message: Rescue from traumatic emotions immediately opens new opportunities.

Sun Focus: Freedom and liberation are important personal themes; you provide others the comfort and support they need.

Affirmation: With action and providence, I surrender fear and guilt.

GEMINI 29
Birthdays: June 18th–20th

Numerology: 89
Sabian Symbol: The first mockingbird in spring
Marc Edmund Jones Key Word: Quickening
Jane Ridder-Patrick Healing Body Point: Fourth rib
Crystal Element: Hessonite
Expression: Hessonite, also known as Cinnamon Stone, is a type of red garnet. Hessonite promotes vitality, self confidence and independence; also acts as a receptor for Divine messages.
Message: Uncover creative potential; live with delightful happiness.
Sun Focus: A natural trendsetter, people emulate you, and sing your praises in the process.
Affirmation: I love new, creative endeavours and the emerging enjoyment they offer.

GEMINI 30
Birthdays: June 20th–22nd

Numerology: 90
Sabian Symbol: Bathing beauties by the sea
Marc Edmund Jones Key Word: Charm
Jane Ridder-Patrick Healing Body Point: Fifth rib
Crystal Element: Larimar (Blue Pectolite)
Expression: Larimar is a semiprecious gemstone variety of pectolite. Spiritually, Larimar has strong Neptune energy; it helps cast off unnecessary emotional layers.
Message: Tranquil enchantment within all environments.
Sun Focus: You have all the virtues a good friend needs, and you set a good example for others to see.
Affirmation: My beauty is without vanity; it reveals spiritual exquisiteness.

CANCER 1

Birthday: June 21st-23rd

Numerology: 91

Sabian Symbol: A furled and an unfurled flag displayed from a ship

Marc Edmund Jones Key Word: Adaptability

Jane Ridder-Patrick Healing Body Point: Sixth rib

Crystal Element: Sphalerite

Expression: The principal ore of zinc, Sphalerite is red iridescence on grey-black crystalline sulphide. Spiritually a guarding stone, it signals loyalty and trust.

Message: Sending clear signs, creating swift and reliable communication.

Sun Focus: You are flexible and confident, inspiring people to redirect and refocus their life course.

Affirmation: I reveal my beliefs, abilities and talents with style.

CANCER 2

Birthdays: June 22nd-24th

Numerology: 92

Sabian Symbol: A man riding a magic carpet over a vast place

Marc Edmund Jones Key Word: Contemplation

Jane Ridder-Patrick Healing Body Point: Seventh rib

Crystal Element: Muscovite Mica

Expression: Muscovite is a phyllosilicate that forms in thin, elastic, transparent, sheet crystals. Muscovite illuminates future plans and personal goals.

Message: Focusing on the horizon; powerful meditation, thought and healing.

Sun Focus: You have a powerful presence, with a unique perspective on individual potential and personal history.

Affirmation: Through meditation and introspection I have reached great heights.

CANCER 3
Birthdays: June 23rd-25th

Numerology: 93
Sabian Symbol: A man all bundled up in fur leading a shaggy deer
Marc Edmund Jones Key Word: Indomitability
Jane Ridder-Patrick Healing Body Point: Eighth rib
Crystal Element: Variscite
Expression: Variscite is a rare, turquoise-coloured, hydrated aluminium phosphate. Variscite promotes courage, understanding and determination in difficult situations.
Message: Preparedness to explore difficult realms.
Sun Focus: Utilising what is at your disposal helps you navigate through life's challenges.
Affirmation: I am invincible; I surmount or circumvent all obstacles before me.

CANCER 4
Birthdays: June 24th-26th

Numerology: 94
Sabian Symbol: A cat arguing with a mouse
Marc Edmund Jones Key Word: Justification
Jane Ridder-Patrick Healing Body Point: Ninth rib
Crystal Element: Cat's Eye (Chrysoberyl)
Expression: Cat's Eye is the clear, green or brown gemstone known as Chrysoberyl. Cat's Eye provides confidence, self-pride, and promotes unconditional forgiveness.
Message: Question the value of exaggerated efforts.
Sun Focus: Exceptional negotiation skills lead to interesting encounters; impressions and reactions are important to understand.
Affirmation: I reason through evidence and patience.

CANCER 5

Birthdays: June 25th-27th

Numerology: 95

Sabian Symbol: An automobile wrecked by a train

Marc Edmund Jones Key Word: Dispersion

Jane Ridder-Patrick Healing Body Point: Tenth to twelfth ribs

Crystal Element: Grossular Garnet

Expression: Grossular Garnet is a calcium-aluminium, green garnet. Grossular Garnet promotes healing and physical wellbeing; use it to avert accidents.

Message: Recognise information, advertising and warning signs.

Sun Focus: You understand the way motion and energy impact our world, and you share this understanding with those you meet.

Affirmation: I understand my decisions have consequence.

CANCER 6

Birthdays: June 26th-28th

Numerology: 96

Sabian Symbol: Game birds feathering their nests

Marc Edmund Jones Key Word: Meticulousness

Jane Ridder-Patrick Healing Body Point: Diaphragm

Crystal Element: Ruby in Zoisite

Expression: Ruby in Zoisite is red corundum surrounded by green zoisite, an epidote mineral. Spiritually, Ruby in Zoisite provides contentment, enchantment and delight.

Message: Facilitating advancement through care and attention.

Sun Focus: You offer those you love considerate and attentive care; you are a sanctuary in this world for others to shelter within.

Affirmation: I will entertain with comfort and generosity.

CANCER 7

Birthdays: June 27th-29th

Numerology: 97

Sabian Symbol: Two fairies on a moonlit night

Marc Edmund Jones Key Word: Ascendancy

Jane Ridder-Patrick Healing Body Point: Thoracic cavity

Crystal Element: Nebula Stone

Expression: A dark black rock with light-green orbicules, Nebula Stone is also known as Eldarite. Nebula Stone enhances an active imagination and supports creative outlets.

Message: Access to unseen astral realms, fairy energy.

Sun Focus: Spending time with like-minded people enhances your enjoyment in life and stimulates magical outcomes.

Affirmation: Joy, happiness and a little frivolity make my life light.

CANCER 8

Birthdays: June 28th-30th

Numerology: 98

Sabian Symbol: Rabbits dressed in clothes and on parade

Marc Edmund Jones Key Word: Appropriation

Jane Ridder-Patrick Healing Body Point: Oesophageal opening of diaphragm

Crystal Element: Pumice

Expression: Pumice is a light-coloured, porous, volcanic rock. Pumice is a neutral stone best utilised when you want to avoid emotional conflicts.

Message: Visible display of uniform beliefs; a sense of belonging.

Sun Focus: You walk the path of least resistance, promoting acceptance and compassion.

Affirmation: I call for abundant energy and style in my life.

CANCER 9

Birthdays: June 29th-July 1st

Numerology: 99

Sabian Symbol: A tiny Miss reaching in the water for a fish

Marc Edmund Jones Key Word: Inclination

Jane Ridder-Patrick Healing Body Point: Pylorus

Crystal Element: Snowflake Obsidian

Expression: Snowflake Obsidian is black volcanic glass with white crystals. Snowflake Obsidian enriches psychic abilities, positive outcomes and confidence.

Message: Bringing matters to the surface with gentleness and compassion.

Sun Focus: You reach out to others, realising that confidence, happiness and calmness play an essential role in life.

Affirmation: I maintain equilibrium through growth and change.

CANCER 10

Birthdays: June 30th-July 2nd

Numerology: 100

Sabian Symbol: A large diamond not completely cut

Marc Edmund Jones Key Word: Latency

Jane Ridder-Patrick Healing Body Point: Fundus of stomach

Crystal Element: Uncut Diamond

Expression: *Diamond* derived from the Ancient Greek means *invincible.* Diamonds cement relationships, represent balance and abundance, and amplify natural talents.

Message: Superlative physical qualities, potent thoughts, and spiritual hope.

Sun Focus: You are a good judge of character; you value and amplify the positive traits of those around you.

Affirmation: I reveal my highest attributes with clarity, patience and care.

CANCER 11

Birthdays: July 1st-3rd

Numerology: 101

Sabian Symbol: A clown doing impersonations

Marc Edmund Jones Key Word: Inimitability

Jane Ridder-Patrick Healing Body Point: Gastric veins

Crystal Element: Chalcopyrite

Expression: Chalcopyrite, also known as Fool's Gold, is a copper ore. Chalcopyrite aids in memory recall and concentration. Echoes the Fool tarot card.

Message: Magnify personal attributes, amplifying feelings.

Sun Focus: You have a great sense of humour; light-heartedness and laughter fill your life.

Affirmation: Everyone wants to laugh; make them laugh.

CANCER 12

Birthdays: July 2nd – 4th

Numerology: 102

Sabian Symbol: A Chinese woman nursing a baby with a message

Marc Edmund Jones Key Word: Materialization

Jane Ridder-Patrick Healing Body Point: Greater curvature of stomach

Crystal Element: Chinese Writing Stone

Expression: Chinese Writing Stone is also known as Porphyry. This stone enhances working with all forms of information, and promotes fairy godmother energy.

Message: Transmission of information, theories, experience, and instruction.

Sun Focus: You are capable and understanding, offering guidance and protection to those around you.

Affirmation: I manifest ideas by translating cryptic symbols into intelligible messages.

CANCER 13
Birthdays: July 3rd – 5th

Numerology: 103
Sabian Symbol: One hand slightly flexed, with a very prominent thumb.
Marc Edmund Jones Key Word: Determination
Jane Ridder-Patrick Healing Body Point: Lesser curvature of stomach
Crystal Element: Shattuckite
Expression: Shattuckite is a beautiful blue, minor ore of copper. Traditionally it radiates spiritual energy, enhancing skills such as prayer and manifesting.
Message: Versatile, tenacious, diligent and persistent.
Sun Focus: You are a multi-skilled, practical person, an achiever.
Affirmation: I know the power of the outstretched hand.

CANCER 14
Birthdays: July 5th-7th

Numerology: 104
Sabian Symbol: A very old man facing a vast dark space to the northeast
Marc Edmund Jones Key Word: Sanction
Jane Ridder-Patrick Healing Body Point: Stomach walls
Crystal Element: Rainbow Obsidian
Expression: Rainbow Obsidian is black volcanic glass with a green-purple sheen. Spiritually, Rainbow Obsidian enlightens self-development and offers protection.
Message: Experience, power and privilege in decision-making and promoting change.
Sun Focus: You have a strong belief in yourself, and you encourage confidence in others.
Affirmation: I have authority and wisdom.

CANCER 15

Birthdays: July 6th-8th

Numerology: 105

Sabian Symbol: A group of people who have overeaten and enjoyed it

Marc Edmund Jones Key Word: Satiety

Jane Ridder-Patrick Healing Body Point: Gastric nerves

Crystal Element: Vesuvianite (Idocrase)

Expression: Vesuvianite is a metamorphic silicate that varies in colour from green to yellow to blue. Vesuvianite enhances loyalty, cooperation and camaraderie.

Message: Variety and abundance, sustaining pleasure, fulfilment and contentment.

Sun Focus: You relish spending time with others; you provide emotional sustenance to friends and family.

Affirmation: I ponder, digest and assimilate all life's experiences.

CANCER 16

Birthdays: July 7th-9th

Numerology: 106

Sabian Symbol: A man before a square with a manuscript scroll before him

Marc Edmund Jones Key Word: Profundity

Jane Ridder-Patrick Healing Body Point: Pancreas

Crystal Element: Bismuth

Expression: Bismuth is a periodic table metal that can form distinct hopper-shaped crystals grown in laboratories. Spiritually, Bismuth is a catalyst for identifying and comprehending complexities.

Message: Perceive, discern, learn and teach prudently.

Sun Focus: You are an intelligently informed person who shares experiences, leading others toward success.

Affirmation: I understand that knowledge leads to experience and insight.

CANCER 17

Birthdays: July 8th-10th

Numerology: 107

Sabian Symbol: The germ grows into knowledge and life

Marc Edmund Jones Key Word: Unfoldment

Jane Ridder-Patrick Healing Body Point: Duodenal opening of pancreatic duct

Crystal Element: Green Fluorite

Expression: Green Fluorite, a type of halite mineral, is naturally fluorescent in ultraviolet light. It develops spiritual and psychic wholeness through love.

Message: Nurtured inspiration germinates, thrives and flourishes.

Sun Focus: Your sense of purpose is strong; you support through knowledge and healing, opening new potentials in others.

Affirmation: I live the process and transformational learning that is life.

CANCER 18

Birthdays: July 9th-11th

Numerology: 108

Sabian Symbol: A hen scratching for her chicks

Marc Edmund Jones Key Word: Provision

Jane Ridder-Patrick Healing Body Point: Duodenal opening of pancreatic duct

Crystal Element: Phlogopite

Expression: Phlogopite is a type of mica, typically light brown in colour. Phlogopite sustains Gaia energy by fostering and protecting those in need.

Message: Through the affectionate fulfilment of needs, relationships are nurtured.

Sun Focus: You provide a safe place for people to rest and recover; your role as provider and carer is very rewarding.

Affirmation: I am empathic and patient; I care.

CANCER 19
Birthdays: July 10th-12th

Numerology: 109
Sabian Symbol: A priest performing a marriage ceremony
Marc Edmund Jones Key Word: Conformity
Jane Ridder-Patrick Healing Body Point: Ampulla of bile duct
Crystal Element: Rose Gold
Expression: Rose Gold is a red-coloured alloy of copper and gold. Rose Gold transforms single entities into a happy union of mind, body and spirit.
Message: Traditional, social and sacred communication, promoting unity.
Sun Focus: Friends look to you to see how they should respond in certain circumstances; they will follow your example.
Affirmation: I pray the development of my ideas leads toward unity and faith.

CANCER 20
Birthdays: July 11th-13th

Numerology: 110
Sabian Symbol: Gondoliers in a serenade
Marc Edmund Jones Key Word: Sentiment
Jane Ridder-Patrick Healing Body Point: Superior pancreatico-duodenal artery
Crystal Element: Ruby
Expression: Ruby is the red variety of Corundum. It is a much sought after, highly valued gemstone. Traditionally, Rubies promote love, devotion and romance.
Message: Amplify affectionate emotions in close relationships.
Sun Focus: You create harmony within personal relationships; you enjoy social gatherings.
Affirmation: I am passionate, vivacious, and filled with love.

CANCER 21
Birthdays: July 12th–14th

Numerology: 111
Sabian Symbol: A prima donna singing
Marc Edmund Jones Key Word: Excellence
Jane Ridder-Patrick Healing Body Point: Inferior
   pancreatico-duodenal artery
Crystal Element: Vanadinite

Expression: Vanadinite is a red, lead-based mineral. Vanadinite promotes
   physical vitality and enhances charisma. It also promotes attentiveness,
   particularly to sound.
Message: Intensify natural talents to influence and entertain others.
Sun Focus: People are attracted to your powerful voice and to what you have to say.
Affirmation: I invite brilliance and fascination into my life.

CANCER 22
Birthdays: July 13th–15th

Numerology: 112
Sabian Symbol: A woman awaiting a sailboat
Marc Edmund Jones Key Word: Equanimity
Jane Ridder-Patrick Healing Body Point: Gastric mucosa
Crystal Element: Avalonite
Expression: Avalonite is a trademark name for a natural coral-peach zoisite.
   Avalonite supports freedom and unconditional love and supports earth
   healing.
Message: Calmly releasing expectations, safe and comfortable in the here and
   now.
Sun Focus: Your calm temperament makes people feel comfortable trusting you
   with their secrets.
Affirmation: I am at one with the universe in every moment.

CANCER 23

Birthdays: July 14th-16th

Numerology: 113

Sabian Symbol: Meeting of a literary society

Marc Edmund Jones Key Word: Criticism

Jane Ridder-Patrick Healing Body Point: Gastric blood vessels

Crystal Element: Thulite

Expression: Thulite is a pink, manganese-rich variety of Zoisite. Traditionally, Thulite enhances sensitivity, imagination, understanding and analysis.

Message: Constructive comments improve performance.

Sun Focus: Compelled to share higher knowledge with others, you enjoy the company of like-minded people.

Affirmation: When the need arises, I judge artfully with propriety and principles.

CANCER 24

Birthdays: July 15th-17th

Numerology: 114

Sabian Symbol: A woman and two men on a bit of sunlit land facing south

Marc Edmund Jones Key Word: Inception

Jane Ridder-Patrick Healing Body Point: Blood vessels of digestive organs

Crystal Element: Rutilated Quartz

Expression: Rutilated Quartz is needle-like, rutile crystals enclosed in Quartz. Spiritually, Rutilated Quartz transmutes negativity and enhances communication with spirit guides.

Message: Initiating and directing timely and appropriate action.

Sun Focus: Your negotiation skills lead you to establishing close friendships and enjoying happy times.

Affirmation: I focus on cooperation and new beginnings.

CANCER 25

Birthdays: July 16th- 8th

Numerology: 115

Sabian Symbol: A leader wrapped in an invisible mantle of power

Marc Edmund Jones Key Word: Destiny

Jane Ridder-Patrick Healing Body Point: Blood vessels of digestive organs

Crystal Element: Magnetite

Expression: Magnetite is black iron oxide with magnetic properties. Magnetite works with spiritual direction and positive choices, and invites Archangel Cassiel energy.

Message: Providence or circumstance, the present moves into the future regardless.

Sun Focus: Your personal charisma guides and inspires others; you are a natural role model.

Affirmation: I modestly carry my own spiritual strength and influence.

CANCER 26

Birthdays: July 17th-19th

Numerology: 116

Sabian Symbol: Reading in the library of a luxurious home

Marc Edmund Jones Key Word: Repose

Jane Ridder-Patrick Healing Body Point: Mammary glands

Crystal Element: Sinhalite

Expression: Sinhalite is a rare gemstone found only in Sri Lanka. Sinhalite works at the highest level promoting spiritual learning through retentive reading and automatic writing.

Message: Peaceful self-awareness and restoration of spirit.

Sun Focus: You face situations with elegant composure and win the respect of others.

Affirmation: I accept peace of mind and relaxation into my life.

CANCER 27

Birthdays: July 18th–20th

Numerology: 117

Sabian Symbol: A storm in a canyon

Marc Edmund Jones Key Word: Intensification

Jane Ridder-Patrick Healing Body Point: Nipples

Crystal Element: Jet

Expression: Jet is a black, organic mineraloid. Jet acts as an insulator against harmful energies, and helps centre thoughts in the present.

Message: Motivation for change; the release of anger, rage and turmoil.

Sun Focus: You can withstand intense situations; you help others to move through difficult experiences.

Affirmation: Extreme emotional force compels extreme transformation and activity.

CANCER 28

Birthdays: July 19th–21st

Numerology: 118

Sabian Symbol: A modern Pocahontas

Marc Edmund Jones Key Word: Compatibility

Jane Ridder-Patrick Healing Body Point: Cartilage of ribs

Crystal Element: Scapolite

Expression: Scapolite is a translucent, metamorphic gemstone. Scapolite highlights individual and collective soul purpose, increases willpower, and inspires activity.

Message: Understand and trust life-path developments.

Sun Focus: You are resourceful and determined; you lead in a pioneering way.

Affirmation: I am strong, kind, original and intense.

CANCER 29
Birthdays: 20th-22nd

Numerology: 119
Sabian Symbol: A Muse weighing twins on golden scales
Marc Edmund Jones Key Word: Value
Jane Ridder-Patrick Healing Body Point: Spleen
Crystal Element: Yellow Gold

Expression: A highly valued precious yellow metal. Yellow Gold alchemically enhances worthiness, purity, beauty and enlightenment, inviting the muses into our midst.
Message: Transforming, valuing, sanctifying golden energy.
Sun Focus: You accurately weigh up situations; you transform darkness into light and hope.
Affirmation: I invite illumination, balance and equity into my life.

CANCER 30
Birthdays: July 21st-23rd

Numerology: 120
Sabian Symbol: A Daughter of the American Revolution
Marc Edmund Jones Key Word: Inheritance
Jane Ridder-Patrick Healing Body Point: Twelfth thoracic vertebra
Crystal Element: Greenstone - Greenschist
Expression: Greenstone is a metamorphic rock rich in chlorite and epidote. Greenstone promotes peace and healing in the immediate environment.
Message: Tradition, history, legacy – transferred gifts aiding progression.
Sun Focus: You see the opportunities and blessings in your life, and share them with others.
Affirmation: I can change the world.

LEO 1

Birthdays: July 22nd–24th

Numerology: 121
Sabian Symbol: Blood rushing to the head due to emotional stress
Marc Edmund Jones Key Word: Irresistibility
Jane Ridder-Patrick Healing Body Point: Left coronary artery
Crystal Element: Brecciated Jasper
Expression: Brecciated Jasper is broken, re-silicified, coloured jasper that has been re-silicified into amazing patterns. Brecciated Jasper directs scattered energy toward life goals.
Message: Calmly re-focus, re-crystallise ideas, create new outcomes.
Sun Focus: You are an emotional person, drawing on personal life experience to generously help others.
Affirmation: My genuine self-confidence is irresistible.

LEO 2

Birthdays: July 23rd–25th

Numerology: 122
Sabian Symbol: An epidemic of mumps
Marc Edmund Jones Key Word: Infection
Jane Ridder-Patrick Healing Body Point: Aorta
Crystal Element: Green Spinel
Expression: Green Spinel is a magnesium-rich gemstone. Green Spinel dissipates emotional discomfort and acts as a conduit to inter-dimensional communication.
Message: Transmit, alter, alleviate, and focus on healing.
Sun Focus: You consciously relate to other people's pain with empathy; you provide sound, helpful, practical advice.
Affirmation: I proliferate empathy as a remedy to help others.

LEO 3
Birthdays: July 24th–26th

Numerology: 123
Sabian Symbol: A woman having her hair bobbed
Marc Edmund Jones Key Word: Decision
Jane Ridder-Patrick Healing Body Point: Right coronary
artery
Crystal Element: Pyrolusite
Expression: Pyrolusite is the name for black, hair-like, manganese crystals. Pyrolusite improves self-image and acceptance through enhancing depth of perception.
Message: Physically transforming, reflecting heart-felt personal choices.
Sun Focus: You evaluate new concepts, eliminate old belief systems, and promote new ideas.
Affirmation: I resolve to be attractive in my physical and spiritual appearance.

LEO 4
Birthdays: July 25th–27th

Numerology: 124
Sabian Symbol: A formally-dressed man with his hunting trophies
Marc Edmund Jones Key Word: Morale
Jane Ridder-Patrick Healing Body Point: Left carotid artery
Crystal Element: Hornblende
Expression: Hornblende is a term applied to common, opaque, black amphiboles. Hornblende promotes seriousness, authority, cooperation and zeal. Orion energy.
Message: Instinctive fulfilment of emotional, physical and survival needs.
Sun Focus: An adventurer, you enjoy risky activities and motivate others to accomplish their goals.
Affirmation: With confidence and purpose I seek out like-minded, successful people.

LEO 5
Birthdays: July 26th –28th

Numerology: 125
Sabian Symbol: Rock formations at the edge of a precipice
Marc Edmund Jones Key Word: Endurance
Jane Ridder-Patrick Healing Body Point: Right carotid artery
Crystal Element: Sandstone
Expression: Sandstone, a quartz-felspar-rich sedimentary rock, often forms highly visible cliffs. Spiritually, sandstone provides enduring strength and energy.
Message: Resilience and enduring strength lead to higher awareness.
Sun Focus: You are a rock of strength and support, enabling others to withstand hardships.
Affirmation: I am blessed with stability of mind from which I have a panoramic view.

LEO 6
Birthdays: July 27th–29th

Numerology: 126
Sabian Symbol: An old-fashioned woman and an up-to-date girl
Marc Edmund Jones Key Word: Contrast
Jane Ridder-Patrick Healing Body Point: Entrance of pulmonary artery
Crystal Element: Peridot
Expression: Peridot is gem-quality forsterite-olivine. Peridot promotes goddess transformational energies, and attracts luck, good health and success.
Message: Engage ancient, contemporary and future traditions, customs and ideals.
Sun Focus: You have the ability to evaluate people and situations, distinguishing and refining the best from what is available.
Affirmation: I am fully self-aware; my status and self-esteem are high.

LEO 7

Birthdays; July 28th-30th

Numerology: 127

Sabian Symbol: The constellations in the sky

Marc Edmund Jones Key Word: Surety

Jane Ridder-Patrick Healing Body Point: Left coronary vein

Crystal Element: Star Sapphire

Expression: Star Sapphires have needle-like, rutile inclusions, which produce a star when cut. A powerful talisman, Star Sapphire acts as a guide and protector.

Message: Constant assurance that planning and navigation are correct.

Sun Focus: A figure of light and hope, you instil confidence in those around you.

Affirmation: I look to the heavens for inspiration and beauty.

LEO 8

Birthdays: July 29th-31st

Numerology: 128

Sabian Symbol: A Bolshevik propagandist

Marc Edmund Jones Key Word: Leaven

Jane Ridder-Patrick Healing Body Point: Inferior vena cava

Crystal Element: Charoite

Expression: Charoite is a purple, Russian, ornamental gemstone. Charoite is emotionally and spiritually uplifting; it integrates ideas within the collective unconscious.

Message: Vision, revolution, loyalty and progression.

Sun Focus: You sympathise with people who have to struggle, which makes you a great friend and confidant.

Affirmation: I use self-expression as an avenue for dramatic change.

LEO 9
Birthdays: July 30th–August 1st

Numerology: 129
Sabian Symbol: Glass blower creating glassware
Marc Edmund Jones Key Word: Deftness
Jane Ridder-Patrick Healing Body Point: Superior vena cava
Crystal Element: Prase
Expression: Prase is the common name for leek-green quartz. Prase reshapes illusion to reveal truth; it encourages originality and harmony.
Message: Skilful ability to manifest beauty and appreciate imaginative influences.
Sun Focus: You are able to create beautiful forms as it is your own spirit that fills the creation and makes it beautiful.
Affirmation: To beautify my surroundings, I invite graceful, skilful craft into my life.

LEO 10
Birthdays: August 1st– 3rd

Numerology: 130
Sabian Symbol: Early morning dew
Marc Edmund Jones Key Word: Rejuvenation
Jane Ridder-Patrick Healing Body Point: Jugular vein
Crystal Element: Cavansite
Expression: Cavansite is a relatively rare, vivid-blue, calcium vanadium silicate. Cavansite enhances personal growth through reflection, and condenses new concepts.
Message: Appreciation of natural and divine cycles.
Sun Focus: You share with friends and family the ideals of simplicity, nature, beauty and love in their purest forms.
Affirmation: I believe in reincarnation; this symbol's timelessness helps me each day.

LEO 11
Birthdays: August 2nd-4th

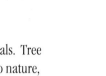

Numerology: 131
Sabian Symbol: Children on a swing in a huge oak tree
Marc Edmund Jones Key Word: Delight
Jane Ridder-Patrick Healing Body Point: Subclavian veins
Crystal Element: Tree Agate / Dendritic Agate
Expression: Tree Agate contains branch-like, black manganese crystals. Tree Agate renews the enjoyment of pleasure, including reconnection to nature, relaxation and carefree play.
Message: Simple pleasures, sharing happiness and friendship.
Sun Focus: Past life sacrifices have paved the way for success in this life – remember to make time to relax and enjoy.
Affirmation: At this moment I am free, joyful, and contented with myself.

LEO 12
Birthdays: August 3rd-5th

Numerology: 132
Sabian Symbol: An evening lawn party
Marc Edmund Jones Key Word: Companionship
Jane Ridder-Patrick Healing Body Point: Vertebral column
Crystal Element: Richterite
Expression: Richterite belongs to the amphibole group of minerals. Richterite enhances interpersonal communication skills, and channels druid energy.
Message: Sociable encounters radiate goodwill.
Sun Focus: Relaxing with friends, entertaining groups, and networking rejuvenate you.
Affirmation: I have wonderful friendships, and happy memories.

LEO 13

Birthdays: August 4th-6th

Numerology: 133

Sabian Symbol: An old sea captain rocking

Marc Edmund Jones Key Word: Retrospect

Jane Ridder-Patrick Healing Body Point: Right ventricle of the heart

Crystal Element: Paua Shell

Expression: Paua Shell is a colourful, iridescent variety of abalone shell. Paua Shells enhance truth and prophesy skills; they contains the wisdom of the ocean.

Message: Gentle, silent reflection; reminiscences.

Sun Focus: You can digest thoughts, impressions and events accurately and nostalgically; you have rich life experience.

Affirmation: I happily share wisdom when I recount personal memories.

LEO 14

Birthdays: August 5th-7th

Numerology: 134

Sabian Symbol: The human soul awaiting opportunity for expression

Marc Edmund Jones Key Word: Ingenuousness

Jane Ridder-Patrick Healing Body Point: Left ventricle of the heart

Crystal Element: Kunzite

Expression: An attractive, pink gemstone, Kunzite is a type of spodumene. Spiritually, Kunzite channels unconditional love, kindness, and intuitive awakening.

Message: Heartfelt honesty, truthfulness and loving emotions.

Sun Focus: You are candid and charismatic; you are receptive to information, people and situations.

Affirmation: I know synchronicity works to support soul connections and karmic ties.

LEO 15
Birthdays: August 6th-8th

Numerology: 135
Sabian Symbol: A pageant
Marc Edmund Jones Key Word: Demonstration
Jane Ridder-Patrick Healing Body Point: Right atrium
Crystal Element: Opalite
Expression: Opalite can be rock that contains small amounts of opal, or man-made glass opal. Spiritually, Opalite stimulates the senses, particularly sight and sound.
Message: Glamorous self-confidence, strongly encouraging new alternatives.
Sun Focus: Your stamina and will help integrate society's exacting standards with ethics and personal happiness.
Affirmation: I believe I am dramatic, sociable, assertive and marvellous.

LEO 16
Birthdays: August 7th-9th

Numerology: 136
Sabian Symbol: Sunshine just after a storm
Marc Edmund Jones Key Word: Recovery
Jane Ridder-Patrick Healing Body Point: Left atrium
Crystal Element: Yellow Fluorite
Expression: Fluorite is a common mineral and can be found in a variety of colours, including yellow. Yellow Fluorite enhances psychic protection, healing and purification.
Message: Symbol of hope, salvation and glory.
Sun Focus: You are generous, confident and loyal, always ready to achieve wonderful things.
Affirmation: I radiate golden energy.

LEO 17
Birthdays: August 8th–10th

Numerology: 137
Sabian Symbol: A non-vested church choir
Marc Edmund Jones Key Word: Communion
Jane Ridder-Patrick Healing Body Point: Right auricle
Crystal Element: Gold Calcite
Expression: Gold Calcite is a gold-coloured, calcium carbonate, crystal element. Gold Calcite illuminates timeless wisdom, holiness and enlightenment.
Message: Common spiritual purpose, belonging.
Sun Focus: Surround yourself with people who share your spirituality and mindfulness.
Affirmation: I give and receive adoration, praise and thanksgiving.

LEO 18
Birthdays: August 9th–11th

Numerology: 138
Sabian Symbol: A teacher of chemistry
Marc Edmund Jones Key Word: Instruction
Ridder-Patrick Healing Body Point: Right cardiac cavity
Crystal Element: Plasma
Expression: Plasma is a popular variety of green chalcedony. Spiritually, Plasma enhances knowledge, information-gathering and guidance – the spirit of the alchemist.
Message: Composition, structure and physical interactions.
Sun Focus: Practical and gifted intellectually, you are motivated to understand the world as we see it.
Affirmation: I believe I will find the answers I seek.

LEO 19
Birthdays: August 10th-12th

Numerology: 139
Sabian Symbol: A houseboat party
Marc Edmund Jones Key Word: Congeniality
Jane Ridder-Patrick Healing Body Point: Ventricular septum
Crystal Element: Green Apatite
Expression: Apatite is a name for a group of phosphate minerals. Apatite promotes strength of character, and rapport within groups.
Message: Compatibility, friendship and happiness.
Sun Focus: Spending quality time with happy, friendly people is fulfilling; enjoy cruising through life.
Affirmation: I take pleasure in life by having fun.

LEO 20
Birthdays: August 11th-13th

Numerology: 140
Sabian Symbol: The Zuni sun worshipers
Marc Edmund Jones Key Word: Fidelity
Jane Ridder-Patrick Healing Body Point: Mitral valve
Crystal Element: Sunstone
Expression: Sunstone is a natural, golden variety of feldspar with hematite inclusions. Sunstone is a leadership stone – it enhances natural life force and magician energy.
Message: Unified solar energy, universal spirit.
Sun Focus: While maintaining a deep respect for natural law, cultural nuances inspire you to explore, learn and teach.
Affirmation: I have a complete and dedicated belief system that works divinely.

LEO 21

Birthdays: August 12th-14th

Numerology: 141
Sabian Symbol: Intoxicated chickens noisily attempt to fly
Marc Edmund Jones Key Word: Accentuation
Jane Ridder-Patrick Healing Body Point: Left atrium
Crystal Element: Aegirine
Expression: Aegirine is a dark green variety of clinopyroxene mineral. Aegirine focuses on ambition, practicality and life goals, liberating unrealised opinions and potentials.
Message: Individual, confident, flamboyant and brave.
Sun Focus: With unrelenting, focused effort, you accomplish the near-impossible with notable success.
Affirmation: I am inventive, determined and quirky, and it works for me.

LEO 22

Birthdays: August 13th-15th

Numerology: 142
Sabian Symbol: A homing pigeon
Marc Edmund Jones Key Word: Enlightenment
Jane Ridder-Patrick Healing Body Point: Left auricle
Crystal Element: Violane
Expression: Violane is a light blue-violet form of diopside. Violane channels true spiritual insight and angelic messages; it connects the everyday to the divine.
Message: Illumination, clarification, focus and perseverance.
Sun Focus: You are on an amazing journey of understanding; continue to relay messages, sharing your experience and wisdom.
Affirmation: I look toward the ascension process to reconnect me to my divine purpose.

LEO 23

Birthdays: August 14th–16th

Numerology: 143

Sabian Symbol: A bareback rider

Marc Edmund Jones Key Word: Audacity

Jane Ridder-Patrick Healing Body Point: Left auricle

Crystal Element: Heliodor

Expression: Heliodor is the gemstone variety of golden-yellow beryl. Heliodor sharpens physical skills and enhances mental attention, and promotes confidence with animals.

Message: Raising the level of perfection, accomplishing more.

Sun Focus: You are dynamic and thrilling; you spend time participating in out-of-the-ordinary pastimes – thoroughly entertaining.

Affirmation: I defy convention. I am daring, bold and adventurous.

♌

LEO 24

Birthdays: August 15th–17th

Numerology: 144

Sabian Symbol: An untidy, unkempt yogi

Marc Edmund Jones Key Word: Imperturbability

Jane Ridder-Patrick Healing Body Point: Papillary muscles

Crystal Element: Sulphur

Expression: Sulphur is a vibrant yellow, natural, crystal element. Alchemically, sulphur is a heavenly element representing passion and free will.

Message: Awareness and tranquillity of the mind–body–spirit triad.

Sun Focus: You have naturally elevated spiritual insight and transcendental powers; others are grateful for your insight.

Affirmation: I remain calm. I am assured all is in Divine order.

LEO 25
Birthdays: August 16th-18th

Numerology: 145
Sabian Symbol: A large camel crossing the desert
Marc Edmund Jones Key Word: Adequacy
Jane Ridder-Patrick Healing Body Point: Pericardium
Crystal Element: Desert Rose
Expression: Desert Rose is the common name for rosette formations of gypsum. It promotes spiritual growth and the awakening of clairvoyant and clairaudient abilities.
Message: Remain centred and confident as ample provisions are available.
Sun Focus: Focused and determined, you have the ability to go the distance, emotionally sustaining others.

Affirmation: I have the nourishment, resourcefulness and endurance to survive.

LEO 26
Birthdays: August 17th-19th

Numerology: 146
Sabian Symbol: A rainbow
Marc Edmund Jones Key Word: Significance
Jane Ridder-Patrick Healing Body Point: Myocardium
Crystal Element: Rainbow Fluorite
Expression: Rainbow Fluorite is a multicoloured, banded fluorite. Rainbow Fluorite acts as a bridge between the physical and the spiritual.
Message: A sign of overwhelming happiness, majesty and security.
Sun Focus: You clearly observe situations and analyse the many parts in the whole, making important discoveries.
Affirmation: I look towards a hopeful, successful and lucky future.

LEO 27
Birthdays: August 18th-20th

Numerology: 147
Sabian Symbol: Daybreak
Marc Edmund Jones Key Word: Genesis
Jane Ridder-Patrick Healing Body Point: Chordae tendinae
Crystal Element: Citrine
Expression: Citrine is a yellow-orange variety of quartz that can occur naturally, or artificially from heat-treating amethyst. Citrine enhances new cycles in life with clear intention and devotion.
Message: New ideas, opportunities, and realizations emerge.
Sun Focus: You bring fresh energy to situations, even the personal and emotional, helping the progression toward success.
Affirmation: The hope that comes with each new day is my inspiration.

LEO 28
Birthdays: August 19th-21st

Numerology: 148
Sabian Symbol: Many little birds on the limb of a large tree
Marc Edmund Jones Key Word: Ramification
Jane Ridder-Patrick Healing Body Point: Chordae tendinae
Crystal Element: Blue Opal
Expression: Blue Opal is un-crystallised, blue-coloured opal. Blue Opal helps ideas flow freely and promotes confidence in interpreting intuitive voices, invites angel energy.
Message: Personal importance, social responsibility, cause and effect.
Sun Focus: You are considerate and accommodating; you enjoy light, familiar social interactions.
Affirmation: I want to share my time and knowledge with people who appreciate me.

LEO 29
Birthdays: August 20th–22nd

Numerology: 149
Sabian Symbol: A Mermaid
Marc Edmund Jones Key Word: Importunity
Jane Ridder-Patrick Healing Body Point: Atrioventricular septum
Crystal Element: Aqua Aura
Expression: Aqua Aura is a man-made, gold-infused quartz crystal. Aqua Aura connects with the divine feminine and esoteric knowledge, enhances Mermaid energy.
Message: Tenacity and aptitude, access to secretive mysteries.
Sun Focus: You are honest, compassionate and faithful, in tune with your personal spirituality.
Affirmation: I shine with enduring inner beauty.

LEO 30
Birthdays: August 21st–23rd

Numerology: 150
Sabian Symbol: An unsealed letter
Marc Edmund Jones Key Word: Confidence
Jane Ridder-Patrick Healing Body Point: Back
Crystal Element: Atacamite
Expression: Atacamite is a vivid green, copper-rich, halide mineral. Spiritually, Atacamite promotes freedom from doubt, and facilitates friendly conversations and correspondence.
Message: Self belief – assurance for future prosperity.
Sun Focus: You communicate from the heart with integrity and passion; others hear your truth, and you are listened to.
Affirmation: I am open, carefree, creative and honest.

VIRGO 1

Birthday: August 22nd-23rd

Numerology: 151
Sabian Symbol: A man's head
Marc Edmund Jones Key Word: Character
Jane Ridder-Patrick Healing Body Point: Duodenum
Crystal Element: Malachite
Expression: Malachite is a banded, green copper carbonate. Malachite amplifies concentration and visualisation skills, promotes emotional growth.
Message: Promote understanding, lucidity and wisdom with gentleness.
Sun Focus: You exemplify dependability, intelligence, analytical insight, and discernment.
Affirmation: I encompass understanding, determination and courage.

♍

VIRGO 2

Birthdays: August 23rd-24th

Numerology: 152
Sabian Symbol: A large, white cross upraised.
Marc Edmund Jones Key Word: Glorification
Jane Ridder-Patrick Healing Body Point: Small intestine
Crystal Element: White Gold
Expression: White Gold is a metallic alloy. White Gold supports the collective ascension process, providing a continual flow of light, alchemically transformational.
Message: Radiant beauty, honour and admiration. Meditate with the divine.
Sun Focus: Positive reputation and personal integrity set you apart from others in a distinctive way.
Affirmation: Rejoice, rejoice, and again I say rejoice.

VIRGO 3

Birthdays: August 25th-26th

Numerology: 153
Sabian Symbol: Two Guardian Angels bringing protection
Marc Edmund Jones Key Word: Security
Jane Ridder-Patrick Healing Body Point: Appendix, caecum
Crystal Element: Angelite (Blue Anhydrite)
Expression: Angelite is a blue-lilac, calcium sulphate, sedimentary mineral. Use Angelite to connect with your spirit guides and guardian angels.
Message: Serene, graceful, safe, and abundantly blessed.
Sun Focus: Angels protect and guide you; with this belief you inspire others to have faith that one is never alone.
Affirmation: I ask my guardian angel to light, guide, and guard my way.

VIRGO 4

Birthdays: August 26th-28th

Numerology: 154
Sabian Symbol: Children from many cultures playing together
Marc Edmund Jones Key Word: Intimacy
Jane Ridder-Patrick Healing Body Point: Ascending colon
Crystal Element: Black Zebra Marble
Expression: Black Zebra Marble is black marble with white veining. This rock enhances communication skills when dealing with diversity in culture, race, gender or ideology.
Message: Limitless creativity and pure fun promote togetherness.
Sun Focus: Your kindness and confidence perpetuate harmony. Surrounded by friends, you are loved.
Affirmation: I promote togetherness, enjoyment and harmony.

VIRGO 5

Birthdays: August 27th-29th

Numerology: 155

Sabian Symbol: A man dreaming of fairies

Marc Edmund Jones Key Word: Outlook

Jane Ridder-Patrick Healing Body Point: Transverse colon

Crystal Element: Ruby Kyanite Fuchsite

Expression: Ruby with Kyanite and Fuchsite is a naturally-occurring rock. This crystal element acts as a bridge between the present and the future, what is and what might be.

Message: A visionary spirit supports uplifting beliefs.

Sun Focus: Original and dynamic, you gain knowledge from the mystic unconscious and express that information creatively.

Affirmation: The power of my imagination banishes fear and promotes hope.

♍

VIRGO 6

Birthdays: August 28th-30th

Numerology: 156

Sabian Symbol: A merry-go-round

Marc Edmund Jones Key Word: Diversion

Jane Ridder-Patrick Healing Body Point: Descending colon

Crystal Element: Cassiterite

Expression: Cassiterite is a tin oxide mineral. Cassiterite promotes enjoyment and optimism in group situations, acting as a shield of protection.

Message: It is child's play, an escapade, innocence giving birth to great wisdom.

Sun Focus: You support the soul's journey through creating and supporting wonder and excitement.

Affirmation: My life is filled with joy, merriment and delight.

VIRGO 7

Birthdays: August 29th-31st

Numerology: 157
Sabian Symbol: A harem
Marc Edmund Jones Key Word: Restraint
Jane Ridder-Patrick Healing Body Point: Rectum
Crystal Element: Freshwater Pearls
Expression: Freshwater Pearls are cultivated in lakes and rivers. Freshwater Pearls promote reverence for women's secret rituals, and accentuate aura colours.
Message: Enhance sincerity and loyalty; focus on emotional truths.
Sun Focus: You transfix people with your natural charm and artistic talents.
Affirmation: I feel like I belong. I am confident people will accept me for who I am.

VIRGO 8

Birthdays: August 30th-September 1st

Numerology: 158
Sabian Symbol: First dancing instruction
Marc Edmund Jones Key Word: Assistance
Jane Ridder-Patrick Healing Body Point: Abdominal cavity
Crystal Element: Mangano Calcite
Expression: Mangano Calcite is a pinkish, calcium carbonate mineral. Mangano Calcite alleviates tension and anxiety through balance and self love; it supports the inner child.
Message: Attuned to inner harmony, guided by the divine.
Sun Focus: You effortlessly support and mentor others, promoting an atmosphere of cooperation and respect.
Affirmation: I am filled with grace and soulful beauty.

VIRGO 9

Birthdays: August 31st-September 2nd

Numerology: 159
Sabian Symbol: A man making a futurist drawing
Marc Edmund Jones Key Word: Experiment
Jane Ridder-Patrick Healing Body Point: Right hepatic lobe
Crystal Element: Turritella Agate
Expression: Turritella Agate is a silicified, fossiliferous rock of freshwater
  gastropods. Turritella fosters new time-space connections, and supports
  creativity, intensity and design.
Message: Venture into the future; investigate new ideas; make predictions.
Sun Focus: Your heightened perspective and transference of important ideas
  lead to new realisations for oneself and others.
Affirmation: I feel free to express my genius.

♍

VIRGO 10

Birthdays: September 1st-3rd

Numerology: 160
Sabian Symbol: Two heads looking out and beyond the
  shadows
Marc Edmund Jones Key Word: Intelligence
Ridder-Patrick Healing Body Point: Left hepatic lobe, bile
Crystal Element: Iolite
Expression: Iolite is the gemstone variety of cordierite, and is pleochroic violet
  and smoky-grey coloured. Iolite opens the door to spiritual realms and pro-
  motes mental clarity.
Message: Potent observations tempered by intelligent rational thought.
Sun Focus: You see beyond the facade of human nature and the veils of time and
  space.
Affirmation: I understand, interpret and utilise the information shown to me.

VIRGO 11

Birthdays: September 2nd–4th

Numerology: 161

Sabian Symbol: A boy moulded by his mother's aspiration for him

Marc Edmund Jones Key Word: Exaction

Jane Ridder-Patrick Healing Body Point: Falciform

Crystal Element: Cluster Quartz Crystal

Expression: Cluster Crystals are prismatic, pyramidal-terminated quartz crystals. Cluster Quartz Crystals promote a clear and honest belief system and connection with spirit guides.

Message: Compelling demand for the best outcomes, always.

Sun Focus: You pay careful attention to detail, giving you authority and wisdom to manage specific tasks and situations.

Affirmation: I have a cherished desire for all to go well today.

VIRGO 12

Birthdays: September 3rd–5th

Numerology: 162

Sabian Symbol: A bride with her veil snatched away

Marc Edmund Jones Key Word: Invitation

Jane Ridder-Patrick Healing Body Point: Abdominal aorta

Crystal Element: Marcasite

Expression: Marcasite is a polymorph of iron pyrite and iron sulphide. Marcasite internally balances male–female energy, uncovering fundamental wisdom.

Message: Elect to incorporate lucid thoughts and actions into the everyday.

Sun Focus: You make a significant difference in people's lives by showing them the way to move forward.

Affirmation: I seek the intimate union between self and the divine.

VIRGO 13
Birthdays: September 4th-6th

Numerology: 163
Sabian Symbol: A strong hand supplanting political hysteria
Marc Edmund Jones Key Word: Power
Jane Ridder-Patrick Healing Body Point: Hepatic arteries
Crystal Element: Epidote
Expression: Epidote is a green-black metamorphic silicate mineral. Epidote is used in directing personal power by actively influencing external events.
Message: High self-esteem and confidence in personal skills supersede fear.
Sun Focus: Your personal power is on show; you have the ability to resolve situations through prudent manipulations.
Affirmation: I choose to influence others, campaigning for positive change.

♍

VIRGO 14
Birthdays: September 5th-7th

Numerology: 164
Sabian Symbol: A family tree
Marc Edmund Jones Key Word: Gentility
Jane Ridder-Patrick Healing Body Point: Cystic arteries
Crystal Element: Pink Fluorite
Expression: Pink Fluorite is the natural, pink variety of the mineral fluorite. Pink Fluorite dissolves persistent, unwanted patterns and promotes affection in all relationships.
Message: Remember the fundamentals; share nourishment, a home and love.
Sun Focus: You treat everyone in your social circle with compassion, courtesy and, indeed, like family.
Affirmation: I pray for all of my brothers and sisters. We are all related in the light.

VIRGO 15

Birthdays: September 6th–8th

Numerology: 165

Sabian Symbol: An ornamental handkerchief

Marc Edmund Jones Key Word: Gracefulness

Ridder-Patrick Healing Body Point: 'Bare area' of liver

Crystal Element: Pink Lace Agate

Expression: Pink Lace Agate is a pink and white banded agate. Pink Lace Agate promotes kindness and compassion, and opens our hearts to Archangel Chamuel.

Message: Sophistication, elegance, gentle and serene moments.

Sun Focus: Exuding beauty and charm, you radiate goodwill and considerateness.

Affirmation: I cherish the elegance and beauty in all things.

VIRGO 16

Birthdays: September 7th–9th

Numerology: 166

Sabian Symbol: An orangutan at the zoo

Marc Edmund Jones Key Word: Dexterity

Jane Ridder-Patrick Healing Body Point: Groove for inferior vena cava

Crystal Element: Crocoite

Expression: Crocoite is lead chromate crystallising in bright red-orange clusters. Crocoite prepares the body for skilful physical activity and mental alertness.

Message: Practical attributes: strength, flexibility, charm and intuition.

Sun Focus: You are asked to handle a great deal in life; take advantage of this and become a valuable mentor.

Affirmation: I am engaging, gregarious and playful.

VIRGO 17

Birthdays: September 8th-10th

Numerology: 167
Sabian Symbol: A volcano erupting
Marc Edmund Jones Key Word: Explosion
Jane Ridder-Patrick Healing Body Point: Abdominal muscles
Crystal Element: Apache Tear
Expression: The Apache Tear is a drop-shaped, smoky obsidian. The Apache
Tear unlocks emotion and frees the spirit from lower energies. Gaia energy.
Message: Natural forces persistently forcing drastic change.
Sun Focus: You compel others to open up, bringing to light hidden stories, trans-
forming lives in an instant.
Affirmation: I ask that my life force be strengthened right now.

VIRGO 18

Birthdays: September 9th-11th

Numerology: 168
Sabian Symbol: An Ouija board
Marc Edmund Jones Key Word: Acumen
Jane Ridder-Patrick Healing Body Point: Obliquus
abdominis muscles
Crystal Element: Golden Beryl
Expression: Golden Beryl refers to the pure yellow variety of beryl. Golden beryl
enhances clairvoyant, clairaudient and clairsentient abilities.
Message: Illuminating communication and divination, accessing the astral
plane.
Sun Focus: The thoughtful conversation you offer people becomes a practical
way to understand esoteric principles.
Affirmation: I seek out and understand meaningful messages.

VIRGO 19

Birthdays: September 10th-12th

Numerology: 169
Sabian Symbol: A swimming race
Marc Edmund Jones Key Word: Elimination
Jane Ridder-Patrick Healing Body Point: Oesophageal groove
Crystal Element: Blue Calcite
Expression: Blue Calcite is blue calcium carbonate. Blue Calcite is cooling, relaxing, and ideal for cleansing emotions, belongings and situations. Mermaid energy.
Message: Motivate the psyche to move with the flow of life.
Sun Focus: Diving in and actively exploring your feelings leads to a deeper awareness of your emotions.
Affirmation: Purification is vital to my health and ultimate success.

VIRGO 20

Birthdays: September 11th-13th

Numerology: 170
Sabian Symbol: An automobile caravan
Marc Edmund Jones Key Word: Variety
Ridder-Patrick Healing Body Point: Bile duct
Crystal Element: Elestial Quartz
Expression: Elestial Quartz displays skeletal growth features. Elestial Quartz facilitates self-determination and self-sufficiency, ensuring body, mind and spirit function optimally.
Message: Make plans to journey to your heart, your mind, your soul.
Sun Focus: You encourage people to travel, promoting personal freedom and respect for diversity.
Affirmation: I give myself the freedom to wander, and time to appreciate it all.

VIRGO 21

Birthdays: September 12th-14th

Numerology: 171

Sabian Symbol: A girls' basketball team

Marc Edmund Jones Key Word: Expression

Jane Ridder-Patrick Healing Body Point: Cystic duct

Crystal Element: Boji Stones (Pop Rocks)

Expression: Boji Stones are concretions of pyrite and marcasite and jarosite. Well-known for their physical healing attributes, Boji Stones encourage us to aspire to greatness.

Message: Aim to succeed. Play an important role in inspiring others.

Sun Focus: Your enthusiasm helps you reach important life goals and in doing so you motivate others to reach theirs.

Affirmation: I enjoy playing fair; it shows my true character.

VIRGO 22

Birthdays: September 13th-15th

Numerology: 172

Sabian Symbol: A royal coat of arms

Marc Edmund Jones Key Word: Prerogative

Ridder-Patrick Healing Body Point: Gall-bladder

Crystal Element: Blue Sapphire

Expression: Blue Sapphire is the gem variety of corundum. Sapphire traditionally is considered a sacred stone in many religions, and acts to elevate psychic awareness.

Message: Connecting with ancestry and cultural history recreates personal identity.

Sun Focus: Emblazon, recognise and marshal important symbols as you validate personal identity.

Affirmation: I devote my life to God, the law, the people, indeed to the greater good.

VIRGO 23

Birthdays: September 14th-16th

Numerology: 173

Sabian Symbol: A lion tamer performs fearlessly in the circus arena

Marc Edmund Jones Key Word: Resoluteness

Ridder-Patrick Healing Body Point: Capsule and ligaments of liver

Crystal Element: Yellow Topaz

Expression: Yellow Topaz is a gemstone. Yellow Topaz is a powerful attraction and manifestation crystal, aiding visualization and projection techniques.

Message: Intrepid and daring, agile and skilful.

Sun Focus: Purposeful and diligent, you approach all aspects of life with vigour and gusto.

Affirmation: I enjoy my life – it is the greatest show on earth.

VIRGO 24

Birthdays: September 15th-17th

Numerology: 174

Sabian Symbol: Mary and her white lamb

Marc Edmund Jones Key Word: Artlessness

Jane Ridder-Patrick Healing Body Point: Capsule and ligaments of liver

Crystal Element: Gypsum

Expression: Gypsum is a common, white mineral occurring in deposits. Gypsum radiates purity and innocence, illuminating the divine in simplicity.

Message: Compassionately mirroring ourselves in others, hopeful that it is returned.

Sun Focus: You care, nurture and protect, communicating kindness and love to those you meet.

Affirmation: I invite mutual love and devotion into my life.

VIRGO 25
Birthdays: September 16th-18th

Numerology: 175
Sabian Symbol: A flag at half-mast
Marc Edmund Jones Key Word: Respect
Jane Ridder-Patrick Healing Body Point: Liver
Crystal Element: Black Marble
Expression: Black Marble is a metamorphic rock. Black Marble is transformational, offering a safe passage from low, old patterns to higher, newer patterns.
Message: Aura of responsibility and dependability, deserving of high regard.
Sun Focus: Stylish and understated, you command admiration due to your good reputation.
Affirmation: I release expectations and accept endings in my life.

VIRGO 26
Birthdays: September 17th-19th

Numerology: 176
Sabian Symbol: A boy with a censer
Marc Edmund Jones Key Word: Rapture
Jane Ridder-Patrick Healing Body Point: Abdominal veins
Crystal Element: Moqui Marbles (Limonite Balls)
Expression: Moqui Marbles, also referred to as "Shaman Stones", are ironstone concretions. Moqui Marbles add positive power to prayer, meditation and astral travel.
Message: Silence, devotion, holiness and adoration.
Sun Focus: A strong believer in a Divine higher purpose, you move forward in a profoundly fulfilling way.
Affirmation: A deepening communion with the Divine sustains me.

VIRGO 27

Birthdays: September 18th–20th

Numerology: 177
Sabian Symbol: Grande dames at tea
Marc Edmund Jones Key Word: Aplomb
Jane Ridder-Patrick Healing Body Point: Iliac nerve
Crystal Element: Wollastonite
Expression: Wollastonite is a white, metamorphic, calcium silicate. Wollastonite reflects inner beauty in the outside world, promoting appreciation for the finer thing in life.
Message: Confidence and self-assuredness promote success.
Sun Focus: With poise and elegant composure, you realise true contentment; others respect you.
Affirmation: I show dignity and gentleness in my life.

VIRGO 28

Birthdays: September 19th–21st

Numerology: 178
Sabian Symbol: A bald-headed man
Marc Edmund Jones Key Word: Dominance
Jane Ridder-Patrick Healing Body Point: Hepatic plexus
Crystal Element: Black Spinel
Expression: Black Spinel is a magnesium-rich gemstone. Black Spinel invites the work of mages, wizards and prophets into your life.
Message: Increasing self-mastery leads to heightened awareness.
Sun Focus: You are persuasive, charismatic, and have an unusual amount of social and political know-how.
Affirmation: Great power lies in all of my choices.

VIRGO 29

Birthdays: September 20th–22nd

Numerology: 179

Sabian Symbol: A man gaining secret knowledge from a paper he is reading

Marc Edmund Jones Key Word: Discovery

Jane Ridder-Patrick Healing Body Point: Quadrate lobe of liver

Crystal Element: Heulandite

Expression: Heulandite is a member of the Zeolite Group. Heulandite permits access to the Akashic Records, providing the most helpful and hopeful information.

Message: Study, knowledge, belief, awareness, enlightenment.

Sun Focus: Your patient nature and attention to detail provide access to insight, motivating personal growth.

Affirmation: I can learn about spiritual power and deep wisdom.

VIRGO 30

Birthdays: September 21st–22nd

Numerology: 180

Sabian Symbol: An urgent task to complete, a man does not look to distractions.

Marc Edmund Jones Key Word: Safeguard

Jane Ridder-Patrick Healing Body Point: Hepatic duct

Crystal Element: Eilat Stone

Expression: Eilat Stone is a natural mix of the copper ores malachite, turquoise and chrysocolla. Eilat Stone encourages soulful dedication to the task at hand.

Message: Pray for spiritual protection and ask for guidance in all things.

Sun Focus: You find fulfilment and value in hard work that stirs your curiosity.

Affirmation: I choose to set up clear boundaries. I defend universal truth.

LIBRA 1
Birthdays: September 22nd-23rd

Numerology: 181

Sabian Symbol: A butterfly made perfect by a dart through it

Marc Edmund Jones Key Word: Articulation

Jane Ridder-Patrick Healing Body Point: Renal pelvis

Crystal Element: White Opal

Expression: White Opal exhibits a display of colours within a white to cream body colour. White Opal softens transformation and reconnection to the Divine.

Message: Spectacular play of emotion, spirit, aura and light.

Sun Focus: You observe metamorphosis inherent in life and express this principle clearly to others.

Affirmation: I look to the source of the light to provide illumination.

LIBRA 2
Birthdays: September 23rd-24th

Numerology: 182

Sabian Symbol: The light of the sixth race transmuted to the seventh

Marc Edmund Jones Key Word: Threshold

Jane Ridder-Patrick Healing Body Point: Renal cortex

Crystal Element: Moldavite

Expression: Moldavite is a translucent green, glassy mineral. Moldavite motivates the expansion of consciousness, promoting a rapid evolutionary experience.

Message: An advanced state, new experiences restoring equilibrium.

Sun Focus: By setting free limiting thought processes, you are supporting the planetary ascension process.

Affirmation: I meditate on moving into new spiritual dimensions.

LIBRA 3

Birthdays: September 24th-25th

Numerology: 183

Sabian Symbol: The dawn of a new day with everything changed

Marc Edmund Jones Key Word: Innovation

Jane Ridder-Patrick Healing Body Point: Adrenals

Crystal Element: Yellow Rutilated Quartz

Expression: Rutilated Quartz is macro-crystalline, yellow quartz with visible rutile needles. Rutile needles intensify the natural qualities of quartz. Sun tarot card energy.

Message: Rebirth; choose glory, success, clarity and energy.

Sun Focus: You shed light on difficult problems by developing new concepts; you are a trendsetter.

Affirmation: I let the past go and I embrace today.

LIBRA 4

Birthdays: September 26th-28th

Numerology: 184

Sabian Symbol: A group around a campfire

Marc Edmund Jones Key Word: Amiability

Jane Ridder-Patrick Healing Body Point: Kidney surface

Crystal Element: Fire Opal

Expression: Fire Opal shows flashes of red, orange and yellow within the pale-yellow-to-red body colour. Fire Opal ignites sociability and hospitality, radiates Phoenix energy.

Message: Flames illuminate, warm, colour and ignite awareness.

Sun Focus: A humble leader and honourable friend, you provide companionship, warmth and support.

Affirmation: My inner fire burns bright and true.

LIBRA 5
Birthdays: September 27th–29th

Numerology: 185
Sabian Symbol: A man teaching the true inner knowledge
Marc Edmund Jones Key Word: Affinity
Jane Ridder-Patrick Healing Body Point: Renal pyramids
Crystal Element: Lithium Quartz
Expression: Lithium Quartz is a pink-purple, opaque variety of quartz. Lithium Quartz enhances meditation and awakens the higher self.
Message: Channel information from the source.
Sun Focus: Your abilities lie in teaching, understanding and experiencing. You seek the knowledge to educate.
Affirmation: I choose an altruistic path.

LIBRA 6
Birthdays: September 28th–30th

Numerology: 186
Sabian Symbol: The ideals of a man, abundantly crystallized.
Marc Edmund Jones Key Word: Personification
Jane Ridder-Patrick Healing Body Point: Pubis
Crystal Element: Lazulite
Expression: Lazulite is an azure-blue, relatively rare magnesium hydroxide. Lazulite clarifies thought processes and promotes confidence to explore new ideas.
Message: Through originality and innovation, conceive and materialise.
Sun Focus: You are open-minded and confident, allowing various thought processes to come together.
Affirmation: I crystallize my life.

LIBRA 7

Birthdays: September 29th–October 1st

Numerology: 187

Sabian Symbol: A woman feeding chickens and protecting them from the hawks

Marc Edmund Jones Key Word: Shrewdness

Jane Ridder-Patrick Healing Body Point: Nerve supply to kidney and renal pelvis

Crystal Element: Hawk's Eye or Falcon Eye

Expression: Hawk's Eye is grey-blue quartz with fibrous inclusions of crocidolite. Hawk's Eye acts as a link between earth and sky, and promotes courage and stability.

Message: Given a cloak of protection, you are safe and secure.

Sun Focus: You nourish and protect your family, friends, objects, plans and ideals.

Affirmation: I am astute and observant.

LIBRA 8

Birthdays: September 30th–October 2nd

Numerology: 188

Sabian Symbol: A blazing fireplace in a deserted home

Marc Edmund Jones Key Word: Guardianship

Jane Ridder-Patrick Healing Body Point: Nerve supply to kidney and renal pelvis

Crystal Element: Fire Agate

Expression: Fire Agate is a form of quartz containing inclusions of iron oxides that result in a play of fiery colours. Fire Agate reignites passion in committed relationships.

Message: Find security and comfort inside.

Sun Focus: You sustain a constant energy flow in your life to fulfill your needs; your aura glows.

Affirmation: My home is where my heart is.

LIBRA 9
Birthdays: October 1st–3rd

Numerology: 189
Sabian Symbol: Three old masters hanging in an art gallery
Marc Edmund Jones Key Word: Accord
Jane Ridder-Patrick Healing Body Point: Nerve supply to
kidney and renal pelvis
Crystal Element: Picasso Jasper
Expression: Picasso Jasper is metamorphic limestone. Picasso Jasper acts as a
map to transformation, leading to a renaissance of spirit in pursuit of life's
purpose.
Message: Uncover the masterpiece of the soul; embody this beauty.
Sun Focus: You are artistic, refined and elegant; people are naturally attracted to
you.
Affirmation: I observe aesthetic and philosophical revelations daily.

LIBRA 10
Birthdays: October 2nd–4th

Numerology: 190
Sabian Symbol: A canoe approaching safety through
dangerous waters
Marc Edmund Jones Key Word: Competency
Jane Ridder-Patrick Healing Body Point: Nerve supply to kidney and renal
pelvis
Crystal Element: Indicolite
Expression: Indicolite is the blue variety of elbaite tourmaline. Indicolite
encourages the use of psychic awareness to gain emotional balance and
self-determination.
Message: Independent, skilful navigation through the unconscious.
Sun Focus: You promote confidence in others by helping them through difficult
times.
Affirmation: I am safe and sound.

LIBRA 11

Birthdays: October 3rd–5th

Numerology: 191
Sabian Symbol: A professor peering over his glasses
Marc Edmund Jones Key Word: Specialization
Jane Ridder-Patrick Healing Body Point: Nerve supply to
kidney and renal pelvis
Crystal Element: Ilmenite Quartz
Expression: Ilmenite Quartz contains ilmenite inclusions. Ilmenite Quartz
outlines important symbols (geoglyphs) and concepts (sacred geometry). Owl
totem.
Message: Advice, guidance, knowledge, higher learning and wisdom.
Sun Focus: Insightful, interesting and instructive, you are respected for your
natural teaching abilities.
Affirmation: I transfer my knowledge and wisdom to others.

LIBRA 12

Birthdays: October 4th–6th

Numerology: 192
Sabian Symbol: Miners emerging from a mine
Marc Edmund Jones Key Word: Escape
Jane Ridder-Patrick Healing Body Point: Left renal system
Crystal Element: Azurite-Malachite
Expression: Azurite and Malachite are blue- and green-coloured copper
carbonates. The Azurite-Malachite blend opens the way to realizing the
unknown.
Message: Truth bearing spiritual wisdom frees the spirit.
Sun Focus: You have an uncanny ability to uncover essential truths; you shed
light on issues from which others hide.
Affirmation: I am prepared to work hard and claim the rewards.

LIBRA 13
Birthdays: October 5th–7th

Numerology: 193
Sabian Symbol: Children blowing soap bubbles
Marc Edmund Jones Key Word: Enchantment
Jane Ridder-Patrick Healing Body Point: Right renal
  system
Crystal Element: Strawberry Quartz
Expression: Strawberry Quartz has red hematite inclusions. Strawberry Quartz
  promotes heartfelt merriment, fun, joy and delight.
Message: Be inspired to live a magical life.
Sun Focus: You simply help make life fun by captivating people with your
  playful, spontaneous and creative talents.
Affirmation: I am living an enchanted life, daily.

LIBRA 14
Birthdays: October 6th–8th

Numerology: 194
Sabian Symbol: A noon siesta
Marc Edmund Jones Key Word: Recuperation
Jane Ridder-Patrick Healing Body Point: Left inguinal
  lymph nodes
Crystal Element: Green Apophyllite
Expression: Green Apophyllite is a transparent phyllosilicate zeolite. Green
  Apophyllite is traditionally a healing crystal bringing growth, renewal and
  recovery in illness.
Message: Regain strength, encourage healing, rest.
Sun Focus: You promote a balance between work and play; maintaining that
  relaxation is essential to everyone's well-being.
Affirmation: Meditation and prayer refresh and reinvigorate my spirit.

LIBRA 15
Birthdays: October 7th-9th

Numerology: 195
Sabian Symbol: Circular paths
Marc Edmund Jones Key Word: Congruity
Jane Ridder-Patrick Healing Body Point: Right inguinal
lymph nodes
Crystal Element: Ammonite or Ammolite
Expression: Opalised Ammolite is a fossilised ammonite gemstone. Ammolite
improves the flow of energy or chi, enhancing personal growth and prosperity.
Message: Living with the natural rhythms and cycles of life.
Sun Focus: Throughout life you revisit ideas, places and situations, spiralling
upward toward holistic awareness.
Affirmation: I rejoice in the circle of life.

LIBRA 16
Birthdays: October 8th-10th

Numerology: 196
Sabian Symbol: A boat landing washed away
Marc Edmund Jones Key Word: Respite
Jane Ridder-Patrick Healing Body Point: Renal arteries
Crystal Element: Blue Fluorite
Expression: Blue Fluorite is a naturally-occurring variety of fluorite. Blue Fluorite
promotes inner peace and emotional balance by releasing worry and fear.
Message: Pamper yourself, regain balance and confidence.
Sun Focus: You speak up for yourself and others with a clear voice and a strong
heart.
Affirmation: I feel relaxed and rejuvenated.

LIBRA 17

Birthdays: October 9th-11th

Numerology: 197
Sabian Symbol: A retired sea captain
Marc Edmund Jones Key Word: Relaxation
Jane Ridder-Patrick Healing Body Point: Suprarenal arteries
Crystal Element: White Fluorite
Expression: White Fluorite is a naturally-occurring variety of fluorite. White Fluorite releases the past as it soothes and calms the spirit.
Message: Time out for quiet solitude, reflecting on adventurous days.
Sun Focus: You pass your knowledge and experiences on to others, helping them to successfully navigate life.
Affirmation: I am in control and choose when to chart a new course in my life.

LIBRA 18

Birthdays: October 10th-12th

Numerology: 198
Sabian Symbol: Two men placed under arrest
Marc Edmund Jones Key Word: Consequence
Jane Ridder-Patrick Healing Body Point: Fatty capsule of kidneys
Crystal Element: Californite
Expression: Californite is the green gem variety of Idiocrase. Californite sheds light on the outcome of thoughts, actions, situations and beliefs, and moderates fear.
Message: Release negative and manipulative behaviour patterns.
Sun Focus: Your belief systems are often tested in difficult ways to motivate positive growth and healing.
Affirmation: I may have much taken from me, but they will never take my freedom.

LIBRA 19
Birthdays: October 11th–13th

Numerology: 199
Sabian Symbol: A gang of robbers in hiding
Marc Edmund Jones Key Word: Divergence
Jane Ridder-Patrick Healing Body Point: Calyx major
Crystal Element: Black Tourmaline
Expression: Black Tourmaline (schorl) is the most common variety of Tourmaline. Black Tourmaline breaks up energy blockages and strongly repels negative energy.
Message: A Robin Hood image, re-distributive and alternative.
Sun Focus: You may keep your true talents hidden, not wanting to show off, yet you will be noticed.
Affirmation: I seek seclusion and protection.

LIBRA 20
Birthdays: October 12th–14th

Numerology: 200
Sabian Symbol: A Jewish Rabbi studying
Marc Edmund Jones Key Word: Heritage
Jane Ridder-Patrick Healing Body Point: Calyx minor
Crystal Element: Violet Spinel
Expression: Violet Spinel is a magnesium, aluminium oxide gemstone. Violet Spinel enhances the connection with ancient sources of truth, and amplifies inherited wisdom.
Message: Faith and reverence while performing duties.
Sun Focus: Research, read and study for personal satisfaction and as a bridge for community illumination.
Affirmation: I receive and I accept Divine teachings.

LIBRA 21
Birthdays: October 13th-15th

Numerology: 201
Sabian Symbol: A crowd upon the beach
Marc Edmund Jones Key Word: Exhilaration
Jane Ridder-Patrick Healing Body Point: Renal hilum
Crystal Element: Sea Shells
Expression: Sea Shells are made from calcium-rich organic minerals. Seashells promote wonder and awe, adding iridescent colours to the aura.
Message: Vitality and enthusiasm, with the joy of new experiences.
Sun Focus: You love social events seeing them as an opportunity to entertain, network and enjoy.
Affirmation: I join in with the excitement, entertainment and energy.

LIBRA 22
Birthdays: October 14th-16th

Numerology: 202
Sabian Symbol: A child giving birds a drink at a fountain
Marc Edmund Jones Key Word: Solicitude
Jane Ridder-Patrick Healing Body Point: Renal veins
Crystal Element: Tugtupite
Expression: Tugtupite is a beryllium-rich feldspathoid. Tugtupite invites youthful happiness, elegance, love and magic into your life.
Message: Belief in the goodness of people and future potential.
Sun Focus: You love and support children and child-like people; your care and concern offer them emotional security.
Affirmation: I seek out and find kindred spirits.

LIBRA 23
Birthdays: October 15th–17th

Numerology: 203
Sabian Symbol: Chanticleer saluting the dawn
Marc Edmund Jones Key Word: Fervour
Jane Ridder-Patrick Healing Body Point: Suprarenal veins
Crystal Element: Mookaite
Expression: Mookaite is a fine-grained, silicified, multi-coloured, radiolarian siltstone. Mookaite inspires and energises one to fulfil commitments. Archangel Michael energy.
Message: Radiant energy, insight and optimism, with burgeoning brilliant light.
Sun Focus: Use your clear, loud voice to arouse enthusiasm, integrity and enlightenment in others.
Affirmation: Awaken and invigorate my mind, body and spirit.

LIBRA 24
Birthdays: October 16th–18th

Numerology: 204
Sabian Symbol: A third wing on the left side of a butterfly
Marc Edmund Jones Key Word: Distinctiveness
Jane Ridder-Patrick Healing Body Point: Blood vessels of renal cortex
Crystal Element: Piemontite Quartz Mica
Expression: Piemontite is a manganese-rich epidote. Piemontite lifts spiritual awareness, opening extra dimensions and allowing for curious, creative self-expression.
Message: Beautifully unique, individually designed to evoke the creative vision.
Sun Focus: Oddities are your speciality; utilise you extra abilities to function on higher levels.
Affirmation: Think again; believe nothing is impossible.

LIBRA 25
Birthdays: October 17th–19th

Numerology: 205

Sabian Symbol: Information in the symbol of an autumn leaf

Marc Edmund Jones Key Word: Tact

Jane Ridder-Patrick Healing Body Point: Blood vessels of renal cortex

Crystal Element: Unakite Granite

Expression: Unakite Granite is composed of pink feldspar, green epidote, and quartz. Unakite enhances perception and promotes a steady release of meaningful information.

Message: Open your senses to inspiring messages from spiritual guides.

Sun Focus: Deepened self-esteem and self-awareness through personal growth lead to metaphysical, logical and physical answers.

Affirmation: I experience profound and gentle transformation.

LIBRA 26

Birthdays: October 19th–20th

Numerology: 206

Sabian Symbol: An eagle and a large white dove turning one into the other

Marc Edmund Jones Key Word: Adeptness

Jane Ridder-Patrick Healing Body Point: Vascular system of skin

Crystal Element: Spectrolite

Expression: Spectrolite is a type of Labradorite with strong iridescence. Spectrolite enhances the integration within the psyche between the conscious and unconscious.

Message: Sensational balancing and transformation processes.

Sun Focus: You temper determination with love, and your expert skills focus people on their life path.

Affirmation: I choose freedom and peace in this current situation.

LIBRA 27
Birthdays: October 20th-21st

Numerology: 207
Sabian Symbol: An airplane hovering overhead
Marc Edmund Jones Key Word: Reflection
Jane Ridder-Patrick Healing Body Point: Vascular system
of skin
Crystal Element: Black Hypersthene
Expression: Black Hypersthene is a magnesium, iron pyroxene. Hypersthene acts as a focal point for visualization and as a doorway to the astral plane.
Message: Contemplation, harmony, and peaceful surroundings renew the spirit.
Sun Focus: You enjoy travel, and encourage others to broaden their horizons through a change of perspective.
Affirmation: I accept that I am made in the image of the Divine.

LIBRA 28
Birthdays: October 21st-22nd

Numerology: 208
Sabian Symbol: A man amidst brightening influences, they are angels.
Marc Edmund Jones Key Word: Responsiveness
Jane Ridder-Patrick Healing Body Point: Bladder
Crystal Element: Laguna Agate
Expression: Laguna Agate is an intensely banded and brightly coloured agate. Look to Laguna Agate to inspire hope and communication with all Angels.
Message: Eternal blessings of the universe in every moment.
Sun Focus: Angels are fundamental to your spiritual learning; they will guide you and those who have faith.
Affirmation: I pray for Angels to stay with me and light my way.

LIBRA 29
Birthdays: October 22nd–23rd

Numerology: 209
Sabian Symbol: Humanity seeking to bridge the span of knowledge
Marc Edmund Jones Key Word: Rationality
Jane Ridder-Patrick Healing Body Point: Right ureter
Crystal Element: Uvarovite
Expression: Uvarovite is a chromium-rich green garnet. Uvarovite accentuates precision, understanding and positive awareness, and reactivates the ascension process.
Message: Communicate important, evolutionary, critical information.
Sun Focus: Objective yet forgiving, you are gifted with organizational skills, ambition and the ability to succeed.
Affirmation: I trust my spirit and will; I foster strong connections.

LIBRA 30
Birthdays: October 23rd–24th

Numerology: 210
Sabian Symbol: Three mounds of knowledge on a philosopher's head
Marc Edmund Jones Key Word: Prescience
Jane Ridder-Patrick Healing Body Point: Left ureter
Crystal Element: Amazonite
Expression: Amazonite is a yellow-green to blue-green gemstone variety of microcline feldspar. Amazonite promotes verbal and written wisdom, and equanimity in action.
Message: Genius, alchemical understanding, innovation and skill.
Sun Focus: Gifted with perspective and prudence, you explore realms in the mind and spirit unknown to most.
Affirmation: I open my mind to the wisdom of the ages.

SCORPIO 1
Birthdays: October 23rd-25th

Numerology: 211
Sabian Symbol: A sightseeing bus
Marc Edmund Jones Key Word: Friendliness
Jane Ridder-Patrick Healing Body Point: Urethra
Crystal Element: Zebra Rock (printstone)
Expression: Zebra Rock is banded kaolinite, mica, quartz and hematite argillite. Zebra Rock encourages amicable group dynamics, compassion and cheerfulness.
Message: Adventure, free time, fun and socializing – it's holiday time.
Sun Focus: Spontaneous and optimistic you love experiencing new things, particularly with friends.
Affirmation: I travel through life with my friends.

SCORPIO 2
Birthdays: October 24th-26th

Numerology: 212
Sabian Symbol: A broken bottle and spilled perfume
Marc Edmund Jones Key Word: Permeation
Jane Ridder-Patrick Healing Body Point: Urethral meatus
Crystal Element: Star Ruby
Expression: Star Ruby is red corundum with oriented crystal inclusions. Star Ruby is a potent magical stone offering potent magical protection, devotion and fidelity.
Message: Gain access to natural enthusiasm, generosity, warmth and passion.
Sun Focus: Pleasure, sexuality, sensuality and indulgence create a very exciting life experience.
Affirmation: I release my true essence and infuse my world with spirit.

SCORPIO 3
Birthdays: October 25th-27th

Numerology: 213
Sabian Symbol: A house-raising
Marc Edmund Jones Key Word: Helpfulness
Jane Ridder-Patrick Healing Body Point: Prostate, uterus
Crystal Element: Aegerine
Expression: Aegerine is a black-to-greenish, pyroxene, igneous mineral. Aegerine facilitates cooperation and improvisation within groups.
Message: Flexibility and adaptability are instrumental to getting the job done.
Sun Focus: Enthusiastic and genuine, you have a generous spirit; everyone is your friend.
Affirmation: I enjoy building valuable community spirit.

SCORPIO 4
Birthdays: October 26th-28th

Numerology: 214
Sabian Symbol: A youth holding a lighted candle
Marc Edmund Jones Key Word: Reliance
Jane Ridder-Patrick Healing Body Point: Testicles, right side of uterus
Crystal Element: Lemurian Seed Crystals (Quartz)
Expression: Lemurian Seed Crystals exhibit well-developed horizontal striations. Record Keepers, these quartz crystals promote a sense of oneness and universal knowledge.
Message: Communicate with spirit through prayer, words, action and energy.
Sun Focus: Deeply spiritual and intuitive, you are keen to explore the realms of sacred ritual and ancient philosophies.
Affirmation: I stand in the circle of light and commune with spirit.

SCORPIO 5
Birthdays: October 27th–29th

Numerology: 215
Sabian Symbol: A massive, rocky shore
Marc Edmund Jones Key Word: Stabilization
Jane Ridder-Patrick Healing Body Point: Testicles, left side
   of uterus
Crystal Element: Stromatolite
Expression: Stromatolite is also known as Algae Iron and Fossil Algae.
   Stromatolite promotes balance, strength and determination, inviting Giant
   energy into situations.
Message: Remain grounded through the tides of time and change.
Sun Focus: Honest and dependable, you have a strong sense of duty; you are a
   valuable friend.
Affirmation: I see and appreciate the enduring quality of natural forces.

SCORPIO 6
Birthdays: October 28th–30th

Numerology: 216
Sabian Symbol: A gold rush
Marc Edmund Jones Key Word: Ambition
Jane Ridder-Patrick Healing Body Point: Right epididymus,
   uterine cavity
Crystal Element: Gold in quartz
Expression: Gold in quartz is a natural concentration of gold. Gold in quartz
   promotes prosperity, holds boundless energy, and promotes vitality and
   confidence.
Message: Gain attention and manifest goals into wealthy reality.
Sun Focus: Through exploration you gain wealth for yourself and endeavour to
   help others with your fortune.
Affirmation: I invite prosperity into my prospective future.

SCORPIO 7
Birthdays: October 29th-31st

Numerology: 217
Sabian Symbol: Deep-sea divers
Marc Edmund Jones Key Word: Involvement
Jane Ridder-Patrick Healing Body Point: Left epididymus,
   right fallopian tube
Crystal Element: Ocean Pearl
Expression: Ocean Pearls are layers of aragonite-calcite and conchiolin. Pearls
   bestow limitless spiritual guidance, deep wisdom, and reconnection with
   honest emotions.
Message: Allow inner light to guide through the abyss.
Sun Focus: With enthusiastic energy, you raise awareness by experiencing the
   world too many take for granted.
Affirmation: I realise my true potential.

SCORPIO 8
Birthdays: October 30th-November 1st

Numerology: 218
Sabian Symbol: The moon shining across a lake
Marc Edmund Jones Key Word: Rapport
Jane Ridder-Patrick Healing Body Point: Scrotum, left
   fallopian tube
Crystal Element: Moonstone
Expression: Moonstone is pearly, opalescent, gem-quality orthoclase.
   Moonstone acts to balance emotion, and reconnect with moon phases and
   goddess energy.
Message: Intuition, visions, magic, receptivity.
Sun Focus: Mysterious and secretive, you have an irresistible, magnetic
   personality that powerfully influences others.
Affirmation: I am enigmatic, intense and powerful.

SCORPIO 9
Birthdays: October 31st–November 2nd

Numerology: 219
Sabian Symbol: Dental work
Marc Edmund Jones Key Word: Practicality
Jane Ridder-Patrick Healing Body Point: Sperm duct, vagina
Crystal Element: Magnesite
Expression: Metamorphic in origin, magnesite is a white carbonate. Magnesite enhances intellectual ability, inquisitiveness and accuracy.
Message: Close examination, action, prompt relief.
Sun Focus: You have a skilful, probing mind; others appreciate your skill, sensibility and credentials.
Affirmation: I seek a catalyst to repair and restore wellbeing.

SCORPIO 10
Birthdays: November 1st–3rd

Numerology: 220
Sabian Symbol: A fellowship supper
Marc Edmund Jones Key Word: Fraternity
Jane Ridder-Patrick Healing Body Point: Corpus cavernosum of penis
Crystal Element: Dravite
Expression: Dravite is a magnesium-rich, brown tourmaline, usually found in schists and marble. Dravite enhances honest communication and aids past-life memory work.
Message: Inner ties, connections, synchronicities, sense of purpose and community.
Sun Focus: Reincarnation is possible; you may remember past life ties, contracts and obligations.
Affirmation: Soul groups and karmic connections help clarify my spiritual purpose.

SCORPIO 11
Birthdays: November 2nd-4th

Numerology: 221
Sabian Symbol: A drowning man rescued
Marc Edmund Jones Key Word: Safety
Jane Ridder-Patrick Healing Body Point: Penis, Labia majora
Crystal Element: Goshenite
Expression: Goshenite is one name for colourless beryl. Goshenite mentally and spiritually stimulates alertness, clear boundary setting and perseverance.
Message: Identify the dangers; revive the body and spirit; take time to recover.
Sun Focus: You help people save themselves and you rescue those who can't.
Affirmation: A kind word and well timed advice are life savers.

SCORPIO 12
Birthdays: November 3rd-5th

Numerology: 222
Sabian Symbol: An embassy ball
Marc Edmund Jones Key Word: Display
Jane Ridder-Patrick Healing Body Point: Seminal vesicles
Crystal Element: Blue Diamond
Expression: Blue Diamonds are found as rare natural blue, and as created diamonds. The Blue Diamond promotes glamour, elegance and prestige in social situations.
Message: Exhibition of romance, congeniality, grandeur and aristocracy.
Sun Focus: Your natural enthusiasm and charisma are contagious; you carry yourself with noble style.
Affirmation: I enjoy spellbinding, elaborate and spectacular events.

SCORPIO 13
Birthdays: November 4th-6th

Numerology: 223
Sabian Symbol: An inventor experimenting
Marc Edmund Jones Key Word: Cleverness
Jane Ridder-Patrick Healing Body Point: Vulva, Labia minora, glans penis
Crystal Element: Strontianite
Expression: Strontianite is a fibrous, white, rare, strontium-rich carbonate mineral. Strontianite promotes wisdom, diligence, intellectual and alchemical abilities.
Message: Investigate the interactions between matter and energy.
Sun Focus: You have a natural ability to come up with innovative and appealing ideas that really work.
Affirmation: I know the formula for success.

SCORPIO 14
Birthdays: November 5th-7th

Numerology: 224
Sabian Symbol: Telephone linemen at work
Marc Edmund Jones Key Word: Attachment
Jane Ridder-Patrick Healing Body Point: Foreskin
Crystal Element: Copper
Expression: Pure Copper is a valuable metal. Traditionally, Copper is known for its therapeutic and alchemical properties; it also facilitates honest, open communication.
Message: Swift, articulate transmissions of truth and wisdom.
Sun Focus: You facilitate easy communication and networking, reconnecting people and places.
Affirmation: I develop and maintain clear connections.

SCORPIO 15
Birthdays: November 6th–8th

Numerology: 225
Sabian Symbol: Children playing around five mounds of sand
Marc Edmund Jones Key Word: Naiveté
Jane Ridder-Patrick Healing Body Point: Cowper's glands
Crystal Element: Sand
Expression: Sand can be made of fine grains of silica, limestone, feldspar, gypsum, chlorite and rutile. Sand negates time constraints and social expectations.
Message: From a sand castle to a Buddhist mandala, impermanence is a spiritual truth.
Sun Focus: Generous, affectionate and happy-go-lucky, you enjoy the company of other people.
Affirmation: I live a life filled with compassion, acceptance and simplicity.

SCORPIO 16
Birthdays: November 7th–9th

Numerology: 226
Sabian Symbol: A girl's face breaking into a smile
Marc Edmund Jones Key Word: Acquiescence
Jane Ridder-Patrick Healing Body Point: Right ovary, cochlea of inner ear
Crystal Element: Albite
Expression: Albite is a white feldspar mineral. Albite fosters warm, loving relationships and pleasant social interactions, promoting emotional success.
Message: Beaming compassion and radiating happiness invite kindness.
Sun Focus: Emotionally inspiring, you find it easy to meet and influence people; never underestimate your personal power.
Affirmation: I am an expression of happiness.

SCORPIO 17
Birthdays: November 8th-10th

Numerology: 227
Sabian Symbol: A woman, the father of her own child
Marc Edmund Jones Key Word: Nucleation
Jane Ridder-Patrick Healing Body Point: Testicular lobes,
 left ovary
Crystal Element: Kimberlite
Expression: Kimberlite is an ultramafic, igneous rock, and an important source
 of diamonds. Kimberlite promotes loyalty, emotional maturity and protection.
Message: Committed, productive, diligent.
Sun Focus: Bold and determined, you are confident being self-sufficient, and
 resourceful in helping others.
Affirmation: I am balanced and in control.

SCORPIO 18
Birthdays: November 9th-11th

Numerology: 228
Sabian Symbol: A woods rich in autumn colouring
Marc Edmund Jones Key Word: Fulfillment
Jane Ridder-Patrick Healing Body Point: Vas deferens,
 hymen
Crystal Element: Yellow Tourmaline
Expression: Natural Tourmaline, coloured by trace amounts of magnesium.
 Yellow Tourmaline inspires intellect, self-esteem and enthusiasm.
Message: Harvest abundance; celebrate accomplishments.
Sun Focus: Passionate and intense, you show others how to lead a fulfilling and
 happy life.
Affirmation: I feel satisfied in achieving my desires.

SCORPIO 19

Birthdays: November 10th-12th

Numerology: 229

Sabian Symbol: A parrot listening and then talking

Marc Edmund Jones Key Word: Conventionality

Jane Ridder-Patrick Healing Body Point: Uterine ligaments, Haller's net

Crystal Element: Wardite

Expression: Wardite is a green to bluish-green, or white, phosphate. Wardite nurtures innate intelligence, quick and witty communication, and clairaudience.

Message: Accepting patterns of thought and action, and transferring these insights.

Sun Focus: You listen to the truth, process facts and speak honestly, adding valuable insight to the natural realm.

Affirmation: I hear and share divine messages.

SCORPIO 20

Birthdays: November 11th-13th

Numerology: 230

Sabian Symbol: A woman drawing two dark curtains aside

Marc Edmund Jones Key Word: Daring

Jane Ridder-Patrick Healing Body Point: Ligaments of penis, Bartholin's glands

Crystal Element: Vivianite

Expression: Vivianite is a colourful, hydrated iron phosphate. Vivianite fosters spiritual transcendence, clarity and clairvoyance. Avalonian energy.

Message: Brave and intrepid, uncover personal power through inner wisdom.

Sun Focus: You provide hope to society, revealing much that is important and valuable.

Affirmation: I am moving beyond limitations.

SCORPIO 21
Birthdays: November 12th–14th

Numerology: 231
Sabian Symbol: A soldier derelict in duty
Marc Edmund Jones Key Word: Deviation
Jane Ridder-Patrick Healing Body Point: Sphenoid sinus
Crystal Element: Zoisite
Expression: Zoisite is a green, metamorphic, epidote mineral. Zoisite enhances self-awareness, and promotes energy and attention to just causes and ethical decision-making.
Message: Determine your own path; march in a new direction.
Sun Focus: You live with high morals, stick to what you believe, and expect those you love to have similar beliefs.
Affirmation: I am different and uniquely so.

SCORPIO 22
Birthdays: November 13th–15th

Numerology: 232
Sabian Symbol: Hunters starting out for ducks
Marc Edmund Jones Key Word: Enterprise
Jane Ridder-Patrick Healing Body Point: Ethmoid bone
Crystal Element: Andradite
Expression: Andradite is a green-grey, calcium-iron garnet. Andradite promotes success in business and safety when travelling; invites Orion and Diana energy.
Message: Trust your instincts; remain focused on goals; actively pursue rewards.
Sun Focus: Through practical involvement, you enhance the status and social acceptance of various groups.
Affirmation: I reshape my spiritual landscape as my ascension process expands.

SCORPIO 23
Birthdays: November 14th-16th

Numerology: 233
Sabian Symbol: A bunny metamorphosed into a fairy
Marc Edmund Jones Key Word: Transition
Jane Ridder-Patrick Healing Body Point: Nasal bone,
   fimbria of Fallopian tubes
Crystal Element: Lepidolite
Expression: Lepidolite is a violet-pink, lithium-rich mica. Lepidolite promotes
   successful outcomes, self-confidence and imagination; invites fairy energy.
Message: Spiritual evolution; move into a higher spiritual vibration.
Sun Focus: An adept teacher, you show how metamorphosis through healing
   and learning results in new and magical outcomes.
Affirmation: I encourage transformation.

SCORPIO 24
Birthdays: November 15th-17th

Numerology: 234
Sabian Symbol: Crowds coming down the mountain to
   listen to one man
Marc Edmund Jones Key Word: Appeal
Jane Ridder-Patrick Healing Body Point: Nasal septum
Crystal Element: Meteorite (Iron-nickel)
Expression: Iron-nickel Meteorites form in outer space. Meteorite encourages
   metaphysical pursuits and spiritual communication, aligns one with higher
   truths.
Message: In the name of love, treat others as oneself.
Sun Focus: Recognised for your prophetic words, you present meaning and
   spiritual awareness in the now.
Affirmation: I believe in the power of prayer.

SCORPIO 25
Birthdays: November 16th-18th

Numerology: 235
Sabian Symbol: An X-ray
Marc Edmund Jones Key Word: Investigation
Jane Ridder-Patrick Healing Body Point: Coccyx, Fallopian tubes
Crystal Element: Quartz, with chlorite inclusions.
Expression: Quartz can naturally occur with inclusions of chlorite. Chlorite Quartz Crystals assist in empowerment and clear insight, and are particularly healing.
Message: By naturally observing and assessing, the truth is profoundly revealed.
Sun Focus: Your penetrating stare sees through any person or situation; your initial assessment is usually accurate.
Affirmation: I have valuable insights.

SCORPIO 26
Birthdays: November 17th-19th

Numerology: 236
Sabian Symbol: Indians making camp in new territories
Marc Edmund Jones Key Word: Extemporization
Jane Ridder-Patrick Healing Body Point: Perineum
Crystal Element: Spessartite
Expression: Spessartite is a manganese-rich, orange to reddish-brown garnet. Spessartite fortifies pioneering attitudes, courage and awareness. Phoenix energy.
Message: Drive, motivation, improvisation, inspiration, invention.
Sun Focus: You search for spiritual and humanitarian friendships, and seek out deeper meaning in the things you do.
Affirmation: I create a sacred space to live within.

SCORPIO 27

Birthdays: November 18th-20th

Numerology: 237
Sabian Symbol: A military band on the march
Marc Edmund Jones Key Word: Intrepidity
Jane Ridder-Patrick Healing Body Point: Anus
Crystal Element: Golden Topaz
Expression: Golden Topaz is a hard, golden-orange, silicate mineral gemstone. Golden Topaz increases personal power, confidence, motivation and boldness.
Message: On show, in command, stirring valour, fearless and intense.
Sun Focus: You are strong and proud; by joining forces with others and fighting for good causes, you achieve the greater good.
Affirmation: I have a brave heart.

SCORPIO 28

Birthdays: November 19th-21st

Numerology: 238
Sabian Symbol: The king of the fairies approaching his domain
Marc Edmund Jones Key Word: Allegiance
Jane Ridder-Patrick Healing Body Point: Mucous membranes
Crystal Element: Peruvian Blue Opal (Chrysopal Andean Opal)
Expression: Peruvian Blue Opals are only mined in the Andes mountains. Peruvian Opals promote responsibility, loyalty, friendship and culture. Fairy energy.
Message: A meeting place, a sanctuary, a sacred place, home.
Sun Focus: You have a very vivid imagination and natural psychic ability.
Affirmation: I am at home everywhere.

SCORPIO 29

Birthdays: November 20th-22nd

Numerology: 239

Sabian Symbol: An Indian squaw pleading to the chief for the lives of her children

Marc Edmund Jones Key Word: Effectiveness

Jane Ridder-Patrick Healing Body Point: Vomer

Crystal Element: Nephrite Jade (Actinolite)

Expression: Nephrite is one of the traditional jade minerals. Nephrite brings luck in negotiations and transactions, love, and a long and prosperous life.

Message: Remember justice; protect the welfare of everyone.

Sun Focus: You find it hard to ask for things that are close to your heart; love yourself as you love others.

Affirmation: I create a life that fulfils me.

SCORPIO 30

Birthdays: November 21st-22nd

Numerology: 240

Sabian Symbol: The Halloween jester

Marc Edmund Jones Key Word: Spontaneousness

Jane Ridder-Patrick Healing Body Point: Nasal muscles

Crystal Element: Poppy Jasper

Expression: Poppy Jasper is red and yellow orbicular jasper. Poppy Jasper promotes a positive, joyful outlook, and energises creative action. Reflects the Fool tarot card.

Message: Exuberant self expression and independence.

Sun Focus: You express your energy optimistically and assertively.

Affirmation: I enjoy merriment and amusement in my life.

SAGITTARIUS 1

Birthdays: November 23rd-24th

Numerology: 241

Sabian Symbol: A Grand Army of the Republic campfire

Marc Edmund Jones Key Word: Reminiscence

Jane Ridder-Patrick Healing Body Point: Pelvic bone

Crystal Element: Tiger Eye with Falcon Eye

Expression: Tiger Eye with Falcon Eye has a golden and blue silky lustre. This crystal element enhances ability to see the truth, offer forgiveness, and it provides protection.

Message: I fought for freedom, rights, and have defended peace.

Sun Focus: People appreciate your point of view and company, particularly those who share your passion and interests.

Affirmation: I remember, lest I forget.

SAGITTARIUS 2

Birthdays: November 24th-25th

Numerology: 242

Sabian Symbol: The ocean covered with whitecaps

Marc Edmund Jones Key Word: Irrepressibility

Jane Ridder-Patrick Healing Body Point: Pelvic girdle

Crystal Element: White Agate (Peace Agate)

Expression: White Agate is a variety of banded silica. White Agate enhances universal knowledge, and promotes Mermaid and Atlantean energy.

Message: The continuous swelling of energy and emotion.

Sun Focus: You are cheerful and lively, attracting unusual and eccentric friends and pastimes.

Affirmation: I seek adventure and freedom.

SAGITTARIUS 3

Birthdays: November 24th–26th

Numerology: 243
Sabian Symbol: Two men playing chess
Marc Edmund Jones Key Word: Ability
Jane Ridder-Patrick Healing Body Point: Ischia
Crystal Element: Verdite

Expression: Verdite is a green, fuchsite-rich, ornamental stone. Verdite aids in mental concentration, knowledge retention, precise work and stamina.

Message: Balance, stability, perfection, strategy and success.

Sun Focus: Accurate intuition and an analytical mind give you a distinct advantage in life.

Affirmation: I am gifted with many unique talents.

SAGITTARIUS 4

Birthdays: November 25th–27th

Numerology: 244
Sabian Symbol: A little child learning to walk
Marc Edmund Jones Key Word: Individuality
Jane Ridder-Patrick Healing Body Point: Femur
Crystal Element: Gaspeite

Expression: Gaspeite is an apple-green, calcium carbonate mineral. Gaspeite enhances youthful energy and opens the mind to optimistic possibilities, fulfilling latent potential.

Message: Moving forward with distinctive style and determination.

Sun Focus: Caring and trustworthy, you charmingly express your individualism while supporting the best in others.

Affirmation: I am an extraordinary individual.

SAGITTARIUS 5

Birthdays: November 26th-28th

Numerology: 245
Sabian Symbol: An old owl up in a tree
Marc Edmund Jones Key Word: Normality
Jane Ridder-Patrick Healing Body Point: Right femoral
artery
Crystal Element: Petrified Wood (opalised)
Expression: Petrified Wood is colourful, opalised fossil wood. Petrified wood is grounding and balancing, and supports Owl and Tree totem energy.
Message: Familiar awareness, daily virtue and traditional wisdom.
Sun Focus: You are an enthusiastic and inspirational teacher; you learn much through life experience.
Affirmation: I am a keen observer of life.

SAGITTARIUS 6

Birthdays: November 27th-29th

Numerology: 246
Sabian Symbol: A game of cricket
Marc Edmund Jones Key Word: Sportsmanship
Jane Ridder-Patrick Healing Body Point: Left femoral
artery
Crystal Element: Blue Aventurine
Expression: Blue Aventurine is a type of quartz with fuchsite inclusions. Blue Aventurine inspires good character, integrity, respect and honour.
Message: Exceptional refinement, courage and temperament.
Sun Focus: A team player, you fit in well with groups of people and you know how to have fun.
Affirmation: I respect fair play and excellence.

SAGITTARIUS 7

Birthdays: November 28th-30th

Numerology: 247
Sabian Symbol: Cupid knocking at the door
Marc Edmund Jones Key Word: Allurement
Jane Ridder-Patrick Healing Body Point: Right superficial
   femoral artery
Crystal Element: Paraiba Tourmaline
Expression: Paraiba Tourmaline is a stunning blue, copper-rich tourmaline.
   Paraiba Tourmaline inspires long lasting love and friendship, amplifies Venus
   energy.
Message: Fervent vitality, sensual devotion, playful ardour.
Sun Focus: Attractive and with charismatic charm, you draw positive attention
   from many people.
Affirmation: I invite love into my life.

SAGITTARIUS 8

Birthdays: November 28th-30th

Numerology: 248
Sabian Symbol: New elements forming deep within the
   earth
Marc Edmund Jones Key Word: Composition
Jane Ridder-Patrick Healing Body Point: Left superficial femoral artery
Crystal Element: Mahogany Obsidian
Expression: Originally molten magma, Mahogany Obsidian is reddish,
   non-crystallised silica. Mahogany Obsidian is a protective stone during
   reformation and evolution.
Message: Synthesise, crystallise, integrate, bring structure into existence.
Sun Focus: You love being intimately involved in nature, enjoying and observing
   natural forces.
Affirmation: Earth, air, fire and water elements support me in my life.

SAGITTARIUS 9

Birthdays: November 29th–December 1st

Numerology: 249

Sabian Symbol: A mother with her children walking up stairs

Marc Edmund Jones Key Word: Education

Jane Ridder-Patrick Healing Body Point: Right lymphatic vessels

Crystal Element: Lavender Jade

Expression: Lavender Jade is a natural jadeitite mineral. Lavender Jade stimulates intuition, patience and wisdom, and invites Master Teachers into your life.

Message: Transformation, upward movement, light and achievement.

Sun Focus: You have a deep enjoyment of loving, teaching, and playing with children.

Affirmation: I help others; I am kind and caring.

SAGITTARIUS 10

Birthdays: November 30th–December 2nd

Numerology: 250

Sabian Symbol: A golden-haired goddess of opportunity

Marc Edmund Jones Key Word: Reward

Jane Ridder-Patrick Healing Body Point: Left lymphatic vessels

Crystal Element: Yellow Sapphire

Expression: Yellow Sapphire is gemstone corundum. Yellow Sapphire enhances expansion and good luck while one is being generous to others, Ceres Energy.

Message: Blessings and kindness make for an easier path to follow.

Sun Focus: Fortunate opportunities will lead toward an increase in money, fame or promotion in your life.

Affirmation: I invite abundance and prosperity into my life.

SAGITTARIUS 11

Birthdays; December 1st-3rd

Numerology: 251

Sabian Symbol: The lamp of physical enlightenment at the left temple

Marc Edmund Jones Key Word: Reconciliation

Jane Ridder-Patrick Healing Body Point: Adductor muscles

Crystal Element: Alabaster (Onyx Marble)

Expression: Alabaster is a common name for a calcite-rich, ornamental stone. Alabaster promotes understanding, calmness and enlightenment.

Message: Spiritual thinking and meditation leading to physical growth and ascension.

Sun Focus: Spiritually motivated, you understand and respect all points of view and see they all have a place in the Divine.

Affirmation: The Divine within me honours the Divine in you.

SAGITTARIUS 12

Birthdays: December 2nd-4th

Numerology: 252

Sabian Symbol: A flag that turns into an eagle that crows

Marc Edmund Jones Key Word: Adjustment

Jane Ridder-Patrick Healing Body Point: Long saphenous veins

Crystal Element: Diopside

Expression: Diopside, a green pyroxene, is a fundamental rock-forming mineral. Diopside enhances adaptability and expansion in personal and spiritual will, Eagle Totem energy.

Message: Signs and messages transforming in sound and vision.

Sun Focus: You are an inspirational leader with a desire for exploration and adventure; you lead by example.

Affirmation: I am adaptable.

SAGITTARIUS 13

Birthdays: December 3rd–5th

Numerology: 253
Sabian Symbol: A widow's past brought to light
Marc Edmund Jones Key Word: Rectification
Jane Ridder-Patrick Healing Body Point: Long saphenous
veins
Crystal Element: Yellow Calcite
Expression: Yellow Calcite is calcite with iron oxide coloration. Yellow Calcite is used for emotional cleansing, resolving childhood fears, and assimilation.
Message: Empowerment, renewed self-confidence, restoration of personal power.
Sun Focus: Your empathetic counselling abilities lead to healing, forgiveness, and release of pain.
Affirmation: I move decisively forward into the light.

SAGITTARIUS 14

Birthdays: December 4th–6th

Numerology: 254
Sabian Symbol: The Pyramids and the Sphinx
Marc Edmund Jones Key Word: Certification
Jane Ridder-Patrick Healing Body Point: Cutaneous vessels
of the thighs
Crystal Element: Lapis Lazuli
Expression: Lapis Lazuli is sodalite-lazurite-rich rock with pyrite inclusions. Lapis Lazuli qualifies intuition, strengthens the mind, and promotes spiritual evolution.
Message: Raise your vibration; align yourself with your higher purpose.
Sun Focus: You are officially recognised in an important capacity due to the valuable insights you communicate.
Affirmation: I am a living reminder that great symbols endure.

SAGITTARIUS 15

Birthdays: December 5th-7th

Numerology: 255

Sabian Symbol: The ground hog looking for its shadow

Marc Edmund Jones Key Word: Reassurance

Jane Ridder-Patrick Healing Body Point: Right iliac vein

Crystal Element: Siderite

Expression: Siderite is a yellowish iron carbonate mineral. Siderite supports courage, insight, confidence and friendship, and invites animal familiars into your life.

Message: Comfort is found freely in faith, hope and love.

Sun Focus: You see meaning in symbols and signs; you 'forecast' and anticipate many outcomes accurately.

Affirmation: I am a natural visionary.

SAGITTARIUS 16

Birthdays: December 6th-8th

Numerology: 226

Sabian Symbol: Seagulls watching a ship

Marc Edmund Jones Key Word: Alertness

Jane Ridder-Patrick Healing Body Point: Left iliac vein

Crystal Element: Hemimorphite

Expression: Hemimorphite is a minor ore of zinc. Hemimorphite supports normal appetite and reduces mental and spiritual fatigue.

Message: Balance a carefree attitude with a responsible nature.

Sun Focus: You have a versatile, easy-going nature; you easily make friends and influence people you meet.

Affirmation: I will make the most of every opportunity.

SAGITTARIUS 17

Birthdays: December 7th-9th

Numerology: 257
Sabian Symbol: An Easter sunrise service
Marc Edmund Jones Key Word: Rebirth
Jane Ridder-Patrick Healing Body Point: Sciatic nerve
Crystal Element: Yellow Prehnite

Expression: Yellow Prehnite is a calcium-aluminium phyllosilicate. Yellow Prehnite encourages spiritual transformation and exalted enthusiasm in new beginnings.

Reflection: Joyful illumination, holiness, the promise of renewal, the blessing of love.

Message: You have inner self-confidence, which helps you build firm foundations in your life and achieve your ambitions.

Affirmation: Resurrection is a sign of hope and joy in my life.

SAGITTARIUS 18

Birthdays: December 8th-10th

Numerology: 258
Sabian Symbol: Tiny children in sunbonnets
Marc Edmund Jones Key Word: Innocence
Jane Ridder-Patrick Healing Body Point: Right femur
Crystal Element: Sugilite

Expression: Sugilite is a purple, potassium-lithium-manganese cyclosilicate. Sugilite imparts a sense of purity, softness, bliss, and awe.

Message: Gentleness, trust and purity are essences worth holding on to.

Sun Focus: You are blessed with a child-like view of the world that will not diminish with age.

Affirmation: I see the world through innocent eyes and it is beautiful.

SAGITTARIUS 19

Birthdays: December 9th-11th

Numerology: 259
Sabian Symbol: Pelicans moving their habitat
Marc Edmund Jones Key Word: Frontier
Jane Ridder-Patrick Healing Body Point: Left femur
Crystal Element: Water Agate
Expression: Water Agate is an agate geode filled with water. Water Agate promotes abundance, resilience, self-sufficiency and rejuvenation.
Message: Have faith; you are where you are meant to be.
Sun Focus: You are a pioneer who successfully pushes the boundaries in all areas of your life.
Affirmation: I joyfully embrace new opportunities.

SAGITTARIUS 20

Birthdays: December 10th-12th

Numerology: 260
Sabian Symbol: Men cutting through ice for summer use
Marc Edmund Jones Key Word: Procurement
Jane Ridder-Patrick Healing Body Point: Head of right femur

Crystal Element: Blue Topaz
Expression: Blue Topaz is a popular gemstone. Blue Topaz encourages leadership qualities, willing participation, integrity and trust.
Message: Cooperation and mutual respect lead to added benefits.
Sun Focus: An inspirational leader, explorer and adventurer, you are prepared and will succeed.
Affirmation: I plan ahead and successfully reach my goals.

SAGITTARIUS 21

Birthdays: December 11th-13th

Numerology: 261

Sabian Symbol: A child and a dog with borrowed eyeglasses

Marc Edmund Jones Key Word: Examination

Jane Ridder-Patrick Healing Body Point: Head of left femur

Crystal Element: Biotite

Expression: Biotite is a black, iron-rich mica. Biotite enhances willpower, thoughtful understanding, commitment and optimism.

Message: Study to remember, perform well, and gain recognition for specialised expertise.

Sun Focus: Life skills have taught you to think outside the box and see all the opportunities available to succeed.

Affirmation: When called upon, I remember information with ease and accuracy.

SAGITTARIUS 22

Birthdays: December 12th-14th

Numerology: 262

Sabian Symbol: A Chinese laundry

Marc Edmund Jones Key Word: Seclusion

Jane Ridder-Patrick Healing Body Point: Right trochanter

Crystal Element: Water Opal

Expression: Water Opal is a transparent opal with a gelatinous appearance. Water Opal promotes emotional success, purification and transmutation.

Message: Morality washes away excess, cleanses and enhances virtuousness.

Sun Focus: You find you retreat to quiet places to reawaken your spirituality and enhance personal growth.

Affirmation: I make time for reflection, stillness and silence in my life.

SAGITTARIUS 23

Birthdays: December 13th-15th

Numerology: 263

Sabian Symbol: Immigrants entering a new country

Marc Edmund Jones Key Word: Entrance

Jane Ridder-Patrick Healing Body Point: Left trochanter

Crystal Element: Blue Chalcedony (Agate)

Expression: Blue Chalcedony is a type of blue agate. Blue Chalcedony supports emotional integration, and transition into the spiritual realms.

Message: Access more expansive and inclusive modes of behaviour.

Sun Focus: With a strong sense of personal and spiritual power, you confront and resolve sensitive issues.

Affirmation: I open the door that leads to Ascension.

SAGITTARIUS 24

Birthdays: December 14th-16th

Numerology: 264

Sabian Symbol: A bluebird standing at the door of the house

Marc Edmund Jones Key Word: Fortune

Jane Ridder-Patrick Healing Body Point: Popliteal fossa

Crystal Element: Blue Lace Agate

Expression: Blue Lace Agate is a blue and white banded agate. Blue Lace Agate is an angelic stone, promoting prosperity, longevity and good luck.

Message: Happiness is in the here and now, not in the past, not in the future.

Sun Focus: Generous and inspirational, you have the ability and drive to achieve your goals.

Affirmation: I am open to good fortune in my life.

SAGITTARIUS 25

Birthdays: December 15th-17th

Numerology: 265

Sabian Symbol: A chubby boy on a hobbyhorse

Marc Edmund Jones Key Word: Emulation

Jane Ridder-Patrick Healing Body Point: Condyles of right femur

Crystal Element: Alunite (Alumstone)

Expression: Alunite is the source of the chemical alum. Alunite has a balancing, stabilizing, grounding effect, and invites Unicorn energy into your life.

Message: Energy and movement, youthful spirit, a fantasy-full life.

Sun Focus: Your easygoing, playful nature encourages others to live spontaneously and look on the bright side.

Affirmation: If you believe in me, I will believe in you.

SAGITTARIUS 26

Birthdays: December 16th-18th

Numerology: 266

Sabian Symbol: A flag-bearer

Marc Edmund Jones Key Word: Nobility

Jane Ridder-Patrick Healing Body Point: Condyles of left femur

Crystal Element: Rhodolite

Expression: Rhodolite is a natural blend of almandine and pyrope garnets. Rhodolite promotes vitality, protection, confidence, power and majesty.

Message: Divine inheritance, the courage to claim what is rightfully ours.

Sun Focus: You are well known, and a much loved person; your peers look to you to facilitate positive developments.

Affirmation: I hold myself with dignity and respect.

SAGITTARIUS 27

Birthdays: December 17th-19th

Numerology: 267

Sabian Symbol: A sculptor's vision becoming manifest

Marc Edmund Jones Key Word: Immortalization

Jane Ridder-Patrick Healing Body Point: Gluteal muscles

Crystal Element: White Marble

Expression: White Marble is metamorphosed limestone. White Marble sustains longevity, continuity, and the manifestation of physical and enduring legacies.

Message: A natural ability to create and appreciate artistic accomplishments.

Sun Focus: Motivated by experience, your ideas are cemented into reality; others take notice and admire.

Affirmation: I live through the good deeds I do.

SAGITTARIUS 28

Birthdays: December 18th-20th

Numerology: 268

Sabian Symbol: An old bridge over a beautiful stream

Marc Edmund Jones Key Word: Conservation

Jane Ridder-Patrick Healing Body Point: Right leg muscles

Crystal Element: Green Opal

Expression: Green Opals have a dominant green play of colour. Green Opal unites mind, body and spirit, restoring health and wellbeing.

Message: Fresh and energetic emotions, constructive thought and activity.

Sun Focus: Gentle and kind, you are always there for others when they need help and support.

Affirmation: I promote harmony, balance and inner peace in my life.

SAGITTARIUS 29

Birthdays: December 19th-21st

Numerology: 269

Sabian Symbol: A fat boy mowing the lawn

Marc Edmund Jones Key Word: Participation

Jane Ridder-Patrick Healing Body Point: Left leg muscles

Crystal Element: Green Sphene

Expression: Green Sphene is a titanium-rich gemstone. Green Sphene supports spiritual growth, transformation, encouragement and openness.

Message: Be attentive and observant; contribute and experience.

Sun Focus: You accomplish great things and make it look effortless; your activity promotes new ideas.

Affirmation: I contribute to the greater good.

SAGITTARIUS 30

Birthdays: December 20th-22nd

Numerology: 270

Sabian Symbol: The Pope blessing the faithful

Marc Edmund Jones Key Word: Sanctity

Jane Ridder-Patrick Healing Body Point: Pear-shaped muscle

Crystal Element: Amethyst (Dark purple)

Expression: Amethyst is purple crystalline quartz. Amethyst promotes balance, harmony, purity, healing, spiritual transmutation and piety.

Message: Bestowed in profound reverence, divine blessings are given to all.

Sun Focus: As a leader, you connect to large groups of people. You have the capacity to see the sacred in people, places and situations.

Affirmation: I am blessed.

CAPRICORN 1

Birthdays: December 21st-22nd

Numerology: 271

Sabian Symbol: An Indian chief demanding recognition

Marc Edmund Jones Key Word: Inflexibility

Jane Ridder-Patrick Healing Body Point: Right patella

Crystal Element: Limonite

Expression: Limonite, or Ironstone, is weathered iron oxide. Limonite promotes symbolic and ceremonial communication, is grounding and protective.

Message: Determined resolve to improve circumstances.

Sun Focus: Personal power and respect come from your strength, stability and firmness.

Affirmation: I make my vision a reality; my mission is successful.

CAPRICORN 2

Birthdays: December 22nd-24th

Numerology: 272

Sabian Symbol: Three stained-glass windows, one damaged by bombardment.

Marc Edmund Jones Key Word: Commemoration

Jane Ridder-Patrick Healing Body Point: Left patella

Crystal Element: Serpentine (China Jade)

Expression: Serpentine is a green, rock-forming mineral. Serpentine enhances benevolence, wisdom, sincerity and honour.

Message: Relive and remember; understand history; observe tradition.

Sun Focus: Patient, thorough, rational, logical and clearheaded, you have an excellent memory.

Affirmation: I open myself to light, truth and hope.

ꝏ

CAPRICORN 3

Birthdays: December 23rd-25th

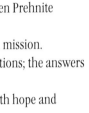

Numerology: 273

Sabian Symbol: The human soul receptive to growth and understanding

Marc Edmund Jones Key Word: Avidity

Jane Ridder-Patrick Healing Body Point: Cutaneous nerves of thigh

Crystal Element: Green Prehnite

Expression: Green Prehnite is a pale-green phyllosilicate. Green Prehnite motivates success, positive growth and transformation.

Message: Spiritual awakening, synchronicity, clearer life-path mission.

Sun Focus: You are receptive to information, people and situations; the answers you seek are found in nature.

Affirmation: I look for inspired answers and am rewarded with hope and wisdom.

CAPRICORN 4

Birthdays: December 24th-26th

Numerology: 274

Sabian Symbol: A party entering a large canoe

Marc Edmund Jones Key Word: Ordering

Jane Ridder-Patrick Healing Body Point: Cutaneous nerves of lower leg

Crystal Element: Purpurite

Expression: Purpurite is a vivid purple, manganese-rich phosphate. Purpurite enhances the spiritual ascension process, along with acceptance, confidence and respect.

Message: Wisdom is incorporating the old and the new.

Sun Focus: You excel at logic and planning, motivating groups into accomplishing great achievements.

Affirmation: I receive lessons as I offer lessons, with kindness and understanding.

CAPRICORN 5
Birthdays: December 25th-27th

Numerology: 275

Sabian Symbol: Indians rowing a canoe and dancing a war dance

Marc Edmund Jones Key Word: Mobilization

Jane Ridder-Patrick Healing Body Point: Cutaneous nerves of knee

Crystal Element: Red Aventurine

Expression: Red Aventurine is quartz with hematite and goethite inclusions. Red Aventurine develops personal power, life-force energy, and revolutionary change.

Message: Co-operation, assertion, strength, respect and purpose.

Sun Focus: You navigate emotions and spirit, consciously utilising energy flow to move toward success.

Affirmation: I honour my personal space and defend my beliefs.

CAPRICORN 6
Birthdays: December 26th-28th

Numerology: 276

Sabian Symbol: A dark archway and ten logs at the bottom

Marc Edmund Jones Key Word: Thoroughness

Jane Ridder-Patrick Healing Body Point: Right adductor muscle

Crystal Element: Black Opal

Expression: Black Opal has a brilliant play of colours within a dark background. Black Opal aids in rebirth, transformation, astral travel, and is a powerful protection stone.

Message: Preparation, skill, stamina and preservation.

Sun Focus: You work without fear, successfully guiding people through their dark times.

Affirmation: I see beyond time; I see into the light.

CAPRICORN 7
Birthdays: December 27th-29th

Numerology: 277
Sabian Symbol: A veiled prophet of power
Marc Edmund Jones Key Word: Supremacy
Jane Ridder-Patrick Healing Body Point: Left adductor
  muscle
Crystal Element: Purple Fluorite
Expression: Purple Fluorite is a popular halite mineral. Purple Fluorite fosters truth, clear intent, wisdom, mystical intensity, and enhances potent spiritual ascendancy.
Message: Divine inspiration, spiritual genius of insight and expression.
Sun Focus: You have tremendous personal power, bestowing guidance to transcend the mundane.
Affirmation: I believe my guides are always with me.

CAPRICORN 8
Birthdays: December 27th-29th

Numerology: 278
Sabian Symbol: Birds in the house singing happily
Marc Edmund Jones Key Word: Establishment
Jane Ridder-Patrick Healing Body Point: Lymph vessels of
  knee
Crystal Element: Danburite

Expression: Danburite is a transparent, borosilicate mineral. Danburite fosters peace, love, gentleness, higher communication skills, and invites Fairies into your life.
Message: Joy, harmony, ecstasy, balance, love and spiritual freedom.
Sun Focus: You are eloquent, youthful and lively; exchanging enlightened ideas is fulfilling.
Affirmation: I connect with my spirit through music and song.

CAPRICORN 9

Birthdays: December 28th-30th

Numerology: 279
Sabian Symbol: An Angel playing a harp
Marc Edmund Jones Key Word: Attunement
Jane Ridder-Patrick Healing Body Point: Nerves of knee
Crystal Element: Euclase
Expression: Euclase is a blue-green gemstone. Euclase inspires creativity, promotes receptivity to intuitive messages, and invites Angels into your life.
Message: Life path, soul purpose, divine spirit and harmony.
Sun Focus: You help others understand angels and the angelic energy at work in their daily lives.
Affirmation: Divine music is my sacred energiser.

CAPRICORN 10

Birthdays: December 29th-31st

Numerology: 280
Sabian Symbol: An albatross feeding from the hand of a sailor
Marc Edmund Jones Key Word: Nurture
Jane Ridder-Patrick Healing Body Point: Right cruciate ligaments
Crystal Element: Chlorite
Expression: Chlorite is a green clay mineral. Chlorite promotes healthy growth, healing, faithfulness, loyalty, independence and good fortune.
Message: Emphatic, sympathetic, gentle, graceful interactions.
Sun Focus: You form strong, supportive, intimate relationships, promoting harmony in your life.
Affirmation: I am nourished by Divine truth.

CAPRICORN 11

Birthdays: December 30th-January 1st

Numerology: 281

Sabian Symbol: Pheasants display their brilliant colours on a vast lawn

Marc Edmund Jones Key Word: Illimitability

Jane Ridder-Patrick Healing Body Point: Left cruciate ligaments

Crystal Element: Eclogite

Expression: Eclogite is a vibrantly coloured, mafic, metamorphic rock. Eclogite aids elucidating patterns and processes, and imparts Master number eleven energy.

Message: Energy, attention, personal power, belief systems without limits.

Sun Focus: Confident, prestigious and successful, you re-create a pathway for positive expansion.

Affirmation: I create the space and freedom for unconditional love to flourish in my life.

CAPRICORN 12

Birthdays: December 31st-January 2nd

Numerology: 282

Sabian Symbol: A student of nature lecturing

Marc Edmund Jones Key Word: Explanation

Jane Ridder-Patrick Healing Body Point: Right knee joint

Crystal Element: Chloromelanite

Expression: Chloromelanite is a natural blend of jadeite and acmite. Chloromelanite unites intelligence, detailed expression, mental capacity and perception.

Message: Respected expertise, validated theory and practical experience.

Sun Focus: You have a logical mind, and place importance on credibility and authority.

Affirmation: I am intelligent, organised and diligent.

CAPRICORN 13
Birthdays: January 1st–3rd

Numerology: 283
Sabian Symbol: A fire worshiper
Marc Edmund Jones Key Word: Magic
Jane Ridder-Patrick Healing Body Point: Left knee joint
Crystal Element: Pyrite

Expression: Pyrite is a common iron sulphide mineral. Pyrite motivates creation through ideas, willpower and desire. It enhances psychic and supernatural abilities.

Message: Desire, illumination, transformation, enlightenment.

Sun Focus: You live with deep spiritual intent, sparking drive and motivation in others.

Affirmation: I affirm clear thoughts, good words, and honourable deeds.

CAPRICORN 14
Birthdays: January 3rd–5th

Numerology: 284
Sabian Symbol: An ancient bas-relief carved in granite
Marc Edmund Jones Key Word: Foundation
Jane Ridder-Patrick Healing Body Point: Right knee cartilage
Crystal Element: Granite

Expression: Granite is an igneous rock containing minerals such as quartz, plagioclase, orthoclase and muscovite. Granite aids the integration of mind, body and spirit.

Message: Recognition, status and prestige, determination to succeed.

Sun Focus: You are hard working, ambitious, responsible and persistent; you achieve long lasting results.

Affirmation: I embrace magnificence, immensity and power in my life.

CAPRICORN 15

Birthdays: January 4th–6th

Numerology: 285

Sabian Symbol: Many toys in the children's ward of a hospital

Marc Edmund Jones Key Word: Abundance

Jane Ridder-Patrick Healing Body Point: Left knee cartilage

Crystal Element: White Howlite

Expression: White Howlite is a calcium-rich, evaporite mineral. White Howlite is an uplifting stone promoting good fortune, abundance, prosperity, comfort and security.

Message: Health, happiness and friendship – these simple pleasures raise the spirit.

Sun Focus: You have a great capacity to show concern, encouragement and affection to those in need.

Affirmation: I am grateful for the abundant goodness in my life.

CAPRICORN 16

Birthdays: January 5th–7th

Numerology: 286

Sabian Symbol: Boys and girls in gymnasium suits

Marc Edmund Jones Key Word: Animation

Jane Ridder-Patrick Healing Body Point: Condyle of right tibia

Crystal Element: Oolite

Expression: Oolite is a sedimentary rock formed from spherical grains. Oolite promotes fitness and a balanced lifestyle.

Message: Peace and happiness in the mind facilitate good health in the body.

Sun Focus: Your invigorating lifestyle stems from beneficial physical activity, meditation and visualization.

Affirmation: Balancing spiritual and physical vitality through play is important to me.

CAPRICORN 17

Birthdays: January 6th–8th

Numerology: 287
Sabian Symbol: A girl surreptitiously bathing in the nude
Marc Edmund Jones Key Word: Immersion
Jane Ridder-Patrick Healing Body Point: Condyle of left tibia
Crystal Element: Iceland Spar
Expression: Iceland Spar is a transparent variety of calcite. Iceland Spar aids mental relaxation, emotional release and spiritual cleansing.
Message: Intuitive, sensual, liberating and exhilarating awakening.
Sun Focus: Artistic and passionate, you enjoy the freedom of natural sensations and an organic lifestyle.
Affirmation: Bathing in water, light and love energises me.

CAPRICORN 18

Birthdays: January 7th–9th

Numerology: 288
Sabian Symbol: The Union Jack
Marc Edmund Jones Key Word: Supervision
Jane Ridder-Patrick Healing Body Point: Ligaments of right knee
Crystal Element: Red Spinel
Expression: Red Spinel is a fine, rare gemstone. Red Spinel enhances camaraderie, enthusiasm, courage, pioneering and survival skills.
Message: Strong, firm, protective, conservative mentoring.
Sun Focus: You have a community-minded spirit, successfully organising various events.
Affirmation: I trust my guides; my spiritual keepers are guarding my way.

CAPRICORN 19

Birthdays: January 8th-10th

Numerology: 289

Sabian Symbol: A child of about five with a huge shopping bag

Marc Edmund Jones Key Word: Expectation

Jane Ridder-Patrick Healing Body Point: Ligaments of left knee

Crystal Element: Plum Agate

Expression: Plum Agate is a type of microcrystalline quartz. Plum Agate supports leadership abilities, wealth, psychic ability, wisdom and generosity.

Message: Anticipate dreams; desires are fulfilling and realised.

Sun Focus: You help others attain the greatness that they may not have seen if not for your insights.

Affirmation: I know Angels come in all shapes and sizes, bearing hidden happiness.

CAPRICORN 20

Birthdays: January 9th-11th

Numerology: 290

Sabian Symbol: A hidden choir singing

Marc Edmund Jones Key Word: Worship

Jane Ridder-Patrick Healing Body Point: Tendons of right knee

Crystal Element: Petalite

Expression: Petalite is a lithium-rich feldspathoid. Petalite resonates with the highest frequencies, opening spiritual awareness and supporting the ascension process.

Message: Unknown, but not empty; out of sight, but not beyond experience.

Sun Focus: You provide hope to those who see no hope; you are a true blessing to those around you.

Affirmation: I use music, reflection, affirmations and candles in prayer.

CAPRICORN 21

Birthdays: January 10th-12th

Numerology: 291
Sabian Symbol: A relay race
Marc Edmund Jones Key Word: Fitness
Jane Ridder-Patrick Healing Body Point: Tendons of left knee
Crystal Element: Covellite
Expression: Covellite is an indigo blue, copper sulphide mineral. Covellite helps support a healthy body, build community spirit, and obtain goals in a timely manner.
Message: Develop energy and expend it with direction and effectiveness.
Sun Focus: You are a health-focused person, inspiring others to be fit and well in all aspects of life.
Affirmation: I share spiritual knowledge with the global community.

CAPRICORN 22

Birthdays: January 11th-13th

Numerology: 292
Sabian Symbol: A general accepting defeat gracefully
Marc Edmund Jones Key Word: Expediency
Jane Ridder-Patrick Healing Body Point: Muscle insertions of upper to lower legs
Crystal Element: Basalt
Expression: Basalt is a black volcanic rock, rich in calcic plagioclase feldspar and pyroxene. Basalt is grounding, strengthening and regenerating for the body and spirit.
Message: Tests of self-worth appropriately fortify my self-confidence.
Sun Focus: A valuable mentor, you have a passion and enthusiasm for learning and sharing knowledge.
Affirmation: One thing I know for sure is that I do not know everything.

CAPRICORN 23

Birthdays: January 12th-14th

Numerology: 293
Sabian Symbol: Two awards for bravery in war
Marc Edmund Jones Key Word: Recognition
Jane Ridder-Patrick Healing Body Point: Muscle insertions
   of upper to lower legs
Crystal Element: Bloodstone
Expression: Bloodstone is a red-green variety of cryptocrystalline quartz.
   Bloodstone fortifies courage, strength, resilience, and inspires leadership abilities.
Message: Expressions of virtue deserve and receive rewards.
Sun Focus: Charming, brave and individual, you are enterprising and free from
   social restrictions.
Affirmation: I gratefully receive acknowledgement and financial reward for my
   work.

CAPRICORN 24

Birthdays: January 13th-15th

Numerology: 294
Sabian Symbol: A woman entering a convent
Marc Edmund Jones Key Word: Consecration
Jane Ridder-Patrick Healing Body Point: Muscle insertions
   of upper to lower legs
Crystal Element: White Onyx
Expression: White Onyx is a banded variety of cryptocrystalline quartz. White
   Onyx amplifies concentration, devotion, and a strong spiritual connection to
   the Divine.
Message: True inner vision, devotion, soul commitment to goodness.
Sun Focus: You belong to a group of people sharing common hopes, dreams and
   lifestyles.
Affirmation: My thoughts pass into new elevated states, creating a Divine
   connection.

CAPRICORN 25

Birthdays: January 14th-16th

Numerology: 295
Sabian Symbol: An oriental-rug dealer
Marc Edmund Jones Key Word: Consignment
Jane Ridder-Patrick Healing Body Point: Connections
between femur and tibia
Crystal Element: Bustamite
Expression: Bustamite is a manganese-rich, metamorphic mineral. Bustamite
promotes enjoyment, recreation, a balanced lifestyle, and an appreciation of
beauty.
Message: A colourful, intricate and splendidly woven life path.
Sun Focus: You have abundant energy and a plethora of persuasive
communication skills.
Affirmation: I am exotic and beautiful; my soul radiates many colours.

CAPRICORN 26

Birthdays: January 15th-17th

Numerology: 296
Sabian Symbol: A water sprite
Marc Edmund Jones Key Word: Restlessness
Jane Ridder-Patrick Healing Body Point: Connections
between femur and tibia
Crystal Element: Chrysocolla
Expression: Chrysocolla is a blue-green, copper-rich mineraloid. Chrysocolla
purifies and renews the self and the immediate environment, and releases
pent up emotions.
Message: Effervescent energy and escapism, lightness of being, freedom.
Sun Focus: You effortlessly deal with your own troubles and help others resolve
their problems.
Affirmation: I am open and accepting of all possibilities.

CAPRICORN 27

Birthdays: January 16th-18th

Numerology: 297

Sabian Symbol: A mountain pilgrimage

Marc Edmund Jones Key Word: Perseverance

Jane Ridder-Patrick Healing Body Point: Deep nerves

Crystal Element: Green Tourmaline

Expression: Green Tourmaline is a vanadium-chrome-rich gemstone. Green Tourmaline connects the spirit to earth energy grid points, increases environmental awareness.

Message: Awareness, strength, empowerment, diligence and passion.

Sun Focus: You have a magnetic personality; you offer people positive alternative perspectives.

Affirmation: I know I can do it; I know I can.

CAPRICORN 28

Birthdays: January 17th-19th

Numerology: 298

Sabian Symbol: A large aviary

Marc Edmund Jones Key Word: Community

Jane Ridder-Patrick Healing Body Point: Right genicular arteries

Crystal Element: Milk Opal

Expression: Milk Opal is a white, transparent to translucent opal. Milk Opal enhances clairaudience, good news, harmony, cooperation, and invites Angel energy into your life.

Message: Collective boundaries support safety and sustainable lifestyles.

Sun Focus: Surrounded by many loved ones, your life is buoyant, fun, exciting and busy.

Affirmation: I stand with my friends and family in the light.

CAPRICORN 29

Birthdays: January 18th-20th

Numerology: 299

Sabian Symbol: A woman reading tea leaves

Marc Edmund Jones Key Word: Signature

Jane Ridder-Patrick Healing Body Point: Left genicular arteries

Crystal Element: Leopard Skin Jasper

Expression: Leopard Skin Jasper is an orbicular jasper. Leopard Skin Jasper aids with interpretation, memory, spiritual discovery and divination techniques.

Message: Symbolism opens pathways; intuition answers questions.

Sun Focus: People confide in you; they see how you empathise with their plight and it comforts them.

Affirmation: I use intuition, feeling, thinking and experience in decision-making.

CAPRICORN 30

Birthdays: January 19th-20th

Numerology: 300

Sabian Symbol: A secret business conference

Marc Edmund Jones Key Word: Opportunity

Jane Ridder-Patrick Healing Body Point: Adductor muscle

Crystal Element: Conglomerate

Expression: Conglomerate is a sedimentary rock cementing rounded cobble and pebble-sized rock fragments. Conglomerate enhances confidence, intellect, wit and charm.

Message: Understand the objectives and plan to realise them.

Sun Focus: Responsible, determined, prudent and aspiring, you make successful life choices.

Affirmation: I make the most of the many opportunities in my life.

AQUARIUS 1

Birthdays: January 19th–20th

Numerology: 301
Sabian Symbol: An old adobe mission
Marc Edmund Jones Key Word: Durability
Jane Ridder-Patrick Healing Body Point: Right tibial nerve
Crystal Element: Aragonite
Expression: Aragonite is a common carbonate mineral. Aragonite facilitates prayerful contemplation, emotional and physical stability, reconnects spirit with the land.
Message: Spiritual growth, strength and permanence.
Sun Focus: You have an interest in different lifestyles, religions and indigenous peoples.
Affirmation: I feel at home in my spiritual life.

AQUARIUS 2

Birthdays: January 20th–22nd

Numerology: 302
Sabian Symbol: An unexpected thunderstorm
Marc Edmund Jones Key Word: Accident
Jane Ridder-Patrick Healing Body Point: Left tibial nerve
Crystal Element: Thunder Egg
Expression: Thunder Eggs are solid, silica-rich, geode stones. Thunder Eggs open the unconscious to higher awareness, intuition and purification.
Message: Sudden and unexpected insights, energy release, flashes of light.
Sun Focus: You are like lightning, striking out different ideas clearly, strongly and passionately.
Affirmation: I respect all the forces that govern my life.

AQUARIUS 3

Birthdays: January 21st–23rd

Numerology: 303

Sabian Symbol: A deserter from the navy

Marc Edmund Jones Key Word: Defiance

Jane Ridder-Patrick Healing Body Point: Right fibula

Crystal Element: Stibnite

Expression: Stibnite is a sulphide of antimony. Stibnite supports strength of character, a free spirit and realistic, commonsense attitudes.

Message: Turn your back, support humanness to attain the greater good.

Sun Focus: You support humanitarian challenges. Proposing ethical opposition, you are a rebel.

Affirmation: I choose to be different, free.

AQUARIUS 4

Birthdays: January 22nd–24th

Numerology: 304

Sabian Symbol: A Hindu healer

Marc Edmund Jones Key Word: Therapy

Jane Ridder-Patrick Healing Body Point: Left fibula

Crystal Element: Blue Apatite

Expression: Blue Apatite is a manganese-rich fluorapatite. Blue Apatite promotes the healing of 'dis-ease', and raises conscious awareness of the physical.

Message: Self-healing, balance and harmony for body, mind and universe.

Sun Focus: You rely on your spiritual centre for solutions; you have divine healing attributes.

Affirmation: I am a natural healer.

AQUARIUS 5
Birthdays: January 23rd-25th

Numerology: 305
Sabian Symbol: A council of ancestors
Marc Edmund Jones Key Word: Antecedence
Jane Ridder-Patrick Healing Body Point: Nerve of right
fibula
Crystal Element: Cacoxenite
Expression: Cacoxenite is a rare phosphate mineral. Cacoxenite enhances astral travel in all time-space directions, and invites spiritual guides into your life.
Message: Call on your ancestors; reconnect and enhance inherited abilities.
Sun Focus: You have a powerful and wise presence; people look to you for guidance.
Affirmation: I look to the wisdom of the past to see more clearly into the future.

AQUARIUS 6
Birthdays: January 24th-26th

Numerology: 306
Sabian Symbol: A performer of a mystery play
Marc Edmund Jones Key Word: Subtlety
Jane Ridder-Patrick Healing Body Point: Nerve of left
fibula
Crystal Element: White Topaz
Expression: White Topaz is a natural, transparent to translucent mineral gemstone. White Topaz promotes the ability to mirror others and our inner self.
Message: Room enough for everyone and everything.
Sun Focus: You show people, in a practical and exciting way, the mysteries of life.
Affirmation: My aura is a subtle energy flowing in me.

AQUARIUS 7

Birthdays: January 25th–27th

Numerology: 307

Sabian Symbol: A child born of an eggshell

Marc Edmund Jones Key Word: Essentiality

Jane Ridder-Patrick Healing Body Point: Right saphenous veins

Crystal Element: Septarian (Dragonstone)

Expression: Septarian is a sedimentary, calcite-aragonite-rich geode. Septarian positively enhances beginnings, fertility, creative potential, quick wit, and clever intelligence.

Message: Genesis, new ideas, new beliefs, new technology and new ways.

Sun Focus: You promote radical ideas and values that become indispensable in the future.

Affirmation: I seek new and inspirational thought patterns.

AQUARIUS 8

Birthdays: January 26th–28th

Numerology: 308

Sabian Symbol: Beautifully-gowned wax figures

Marc Edmund Jones Key Word: Impact

Jane Ridder-Patrick Healing Body Point: Left saphenous veins

Crystal Element: Pink Diamond

Expression: Pink Diamonds are the most rare and valuable diamonds. Pink Diamonds promote inner and outer beauty, open heartedness, and universal love.

Message: Use creativity to visually enhance life.

Sun Focus: A talented verbal and visual linguist, you stand apart from the crowd.

Affirmation: I am beautiful.

AQUARIUS 9

Birthdays: January 27th-29th

Numerology: 309

Sabian Symbol: A flag turned into an eagle

Marc Edmund Jones Key Word: Dramatization

Jane Ridder-Patrick Healing Body Point: Skin of right
lower leg

Crystal Element: Pietersite (Eagle Eye)

Expression: Pietersite is a fibrous, brecciated, blue-gold-red mineral. Pietersite
promotes nobility, pride, fierceness, superiority, courage, and intellectual ability.

Message: True and accurate representations are transformational.

Sun Focus: Your ideas and beliefs mark a substantial and powerful force in this
world.

Affirmation: I am powerful. I achieve greatness.

AQUARIUS 10

Birthdays: January 28th-30th

Numerology: 310

Sabian Symbol: A popularity that proves ephemeral

Marc Edmund Jones Key Word: Approbation

Jane Ridder-Patrick Healing Body Point: Skin of left lower leg

Crystal Element: Ruby in Kyanite

Expression: Ruby in Kyanite is ruby crystal inclusions in green kyanite. Ruby in
Kyanite enhances self-worth, self-acceptance and self-confidence.

Message: True depth of character is not always easily seen.

Sun Focus: An innovative individual, you continually re-invent yourself and your
ideas.

Affirmation: I believe in myself.

AQUARIUS 11

Birthdays: January 29th-31st

Numerology: 311

Sabian Symbol: Man tête-à-tête with his inspiration

Marc Edmund Jones Key Word: Ecstasy

Jane Ridder-Patrick Healing Body Point: Right cruciate ligaments

Crystal Element: Phenacite

Expression: Phenacite is a beryllium, silicate, crystal mineral. Phenacite facilitates visionary intuition, invites Angels and Ascended Masters into your life.

Message: Seek the highest vibration through transcendental practices.

Sun Focus: You broaden human consciousness through writing, meditation and intuition.

Affirmation: I realize my best ideas are born out of inspiration.

AQUARIUS 12

Birthdays: January 30th-February 1st

Numerology: 312

Sabian Symbol: People on stairs graduated upwards

Marc Edmund Jones Key Word: Progression

Jane Ridder-Patrick Healing Body Point: Left cruciate ligaments

Crystal Element: Amegreen

Expression: Amegreen is naturally-banded purple amethyst, white quartz and green amethyst. Amegreen facilitates spiritual and physical evolutionary development.

Message: An esoteric path, the process of ascension, onward and upward.

Sun Focus: Naturally sceptical, you prove things for yourself before moving to a new belief system.

Affirmation: My spiritual progress raises my ability to work with the Divine.

AQUARIUS 13

Birthdays: January 31st–February 2nd

Numerology: 313

Sabian Symbol: A barometer

Marc Edmund Jones Key Word: Indication

Jane Ridder-Patrick Healing Body Point: Right tibial artery

Crystal Element: Ulexite

Expression: Ulexite is a boron-rich carbonate. Ulexite is an amplifying crystal; use it to amplify other crystal energies, natural talents, and in manifesting.

Message: Utilise the tools at hand to forecast imminent change.

Sun Focus: You are a perceptive person, acting as translator of spirit and emotion.

Affirmation: I sense the Divine in everything.

AQUARIUS 14

Birthdays: February 1st–3rd

Numerology: 314

Sabian Symbol: A train entering a tunnel

Marc Edmund Jones Key Word: Courtesy

Jane Ridder-Patrick Healing Body Point: Left tibial artery

Crystal Element: Black Jasper

Expression: Black Jasper is an opaque, impure cryptocrystalline quartz. Black Jasper is a protective stone; it enhances positive, affirmative thoughts and sentiments.

Message: Respect and kindness in the present sets the tone and direction for the future.

Sun Focus: You encourage peace and harmony, promoting the equality of all people.

Affirmation: I am confident I will stay on track to achieve my highest potential.

AQUARIUS 15
Birthdays: February 2nd–4th

Numerology: 315
Sabian Symbol: Two lovebirds sitting on a fence
Marc Edmund Jones Key Word: Affirmation
Jane Ridder-Patrick Healing Body Point: Lymph vessels of right lower leg
Crystal Element: Rose Quartz
Expression: A popular mineral, Rose Quartz is pink-coloured quartz. Rose Quartz promotes love, self love, love between people, and spiritual love.
Message: Love is patient and kind; love rejoices in the truth.
Sun Focus: You show deep affection for people in your life; you radiate hope, joy and harmony.
Affirmation: I believe in the Divine; it is love.

AQUARIUS 16
Birthdays: February 3rd–5th

Numerology: 316
Sabian Symbol: A big-business man at his desk
Marc Edmund Jones Key Word: Accomplishment
Jane Ridder-Patrick Healing Body Point: Lymph vessels of left lower leg
Crystal Element: Azurite
Expression: Azurite is a copper carbonate mineral. Azurite fosters leadership qualities, focus, determination, wisdom and judgement. Invites Archangel energy into your life.
Message: Confidence, competence, self-respect, achievement, self-fulfilment.
Sun Focus: You evaluate, rationalise and integrate intelligently, creating successful systems.
Affirmation: I see how successful my life is today.

AQUARIUS 17

Birthdays: February 4th-6th

Numerology: 317

Sabian Symbol: A watchdog standing guard

Marc Edmund Jones Key Word: Probity

Jane Ridder-Patrick Healing Body Point: Spinal nervous system

Crystal Element: Tiger Eye

Expression: Tiger Eye is silicified, fibrous crocidolite. Tiger Eye is a powerful stone of protection, integrity and strength; it also promotes fortunate outcomes.

Message: Guardianship, self-assurance, loyalty and virtuousness.

Sun Focus: You are intuitively alert to undercurrents, hence you avoid trouble and protect others.

Affirmation: Angels before me, beside me and all around me, protecting me from harm.

AQUARIUS 18

Birthdays: February 5th-7th

Numerology: 318

Sabian Symbol: A man unmasked

Marc Edmund Jones Key Word: Analysis

Jane Ridder-Patrick Healing Body Point: Spinal nervous system

Crystal Element: Tourmalinated Quartz

Expression: Tourmalinated Quartz is quartz with black tourmaline inclusions. Tourmalinated Quartz promotes assertiveness, commitment and cooperation.

Message: Candid acknowledgement of the current situation.

Sun Focus: You uncover fear, resolving complicated problems with empathetic skill and insight.

Affirmation: I confront and resolve sensitive issues.

AQUARIUS 19

Birthdays: February 6th-8th

Numerology: 319

Sabian Symbol: A forest fire quenched

Marc Edmund Jones Key Word: Concern

Jane Ridder-Patrick Healing Body Point: Spinal nervous system

Crystal Element: Amber

Expression: Amber is fossilised resin, containing plant or animal matter. Amber supports a positive path for change, invites Phoenix energy into your life.

Message: Rescuers provide a safe environment; relief is near.

Sun Focus: Your inspirational wisdom helps others understand the consequences of their actions.

Affirmation: My fears are clearly expressed and I expect them to be resolved.

AQUARIUS 20

Birthdays: February 7th-9th

Numerology: 320

Sabian Symbol: A big white dove, a message bearer.

Marc Edmund Jones Key Word: Conviction

Jane Ridder-Patrick Healing Body Point: Spinal nervous system

Crystal Element: Schalenblende

Expression: Schalenblende is sphalerite, galena, zinc, marcasite and wurtzite. Schalenblende promotes confidence and receptivity to divine messages.

Message: Angelic Energy, blessings, confidence, beliefs and sincerity.

Sun Focus: You share your personal truth, providing messages of peace, hope and love.

Affirmation: As I pray, Archangel Gabriel guides me with clear messages.

AQUARIUS 21

Birthdays: February 8th-10th

Numerology: 321

Sabian Symbol: A woman disappointed and disillusioned

Marc Edmund Jones Key Word: Clearance

Jane Ridder-Patrick Healing Body Point: Spinal nervous system

Crystal Element: Bixbite

Expression: Bixbite is the red variety of gemstone beryl. Bixbite releases false expectations, promotes self-worth and self-motivation.

Message: Space and freedom with permission to move forward.

Sun Focus: You are altruistic and visionary, and are able to change situations, people and outcomes.

Affirmation: I increase my personal power through life experience.

AQUARIUS 22

Birthdays: February 9th-11th

Numerology: 322

Sabian Symbol: A rug placed on a floor for children to play

Marc Edmund Jones Key Word: Refinement

Jane Ridder-Patrick Healing Body Point: Right gastrocnemius muscle

Crystal Element: Dumortierite

Expression: Dumortierite is a blue, boro-silicate mineral. Dumortierite promotes companionship, tolerance, and reduces hyperactivity.

Message: Enhance playful and happy times; encourage dormant talent.

Sun Focus: You look to new generations for meaning and clarity; it is child's play.

Affirmation: My life journey is filled with happiness.

AQUARIUS 23

Birthdays: February 10th-12th

Numerology: 323

Sabian Symbol: A big bear sitting down and waving all its paws

Marc Edmund Jones Key Word: Aptitude

Jane Ridder-Patrick Healing Body Point: Left gastrocnemius muscle

Crystal Element: Okenite and/or Mesolite

Expression: Okenite is a fibrous, hydrated calcium silicate. Mesolite is sodium-calcium zeolite. Both crystal elements enhance natural abilities and curiosity, and invite bear totem energy into your life.

Message: Strength, agility, endurance and power.

Sun Focus: You are friendly, happy and inclusive; you have a positive view on all things.

Affirmation: I am beauty in the world. I am happy. I am free.

AQUARIUS 24

Birthdays: February 11th-13th

Numerology: 324

Sabian Symbol: A man turning his back on his passions teaches from his experience.

Marc Edmund Jones Key Word: Serenity

Jane Ridder-Patrick Healing Body Point: Right tibialis anterior muscle

Crystal Element: Graphite

Expression: Graphite is a platy silver form of carbon. Graphite promotes eloquent communication, inspiration, and a focus for intention.

Message: Peace, wisdom and understanding, learned authority.

Sun Focus: Philosophical, you utilise ideas and concepts to help express universal wisdom.

Affirmation: I understand I am a mirror of the world.

AQUARIUS 25

Birthdays: February 12th–14th

Numerology: 325
Sabian Symbol: A butterfly with the right wing more perfectly formed
Marc Edmund Jones Key Word: Uniqueness
Jane Ridder-Patrick Healing Body Point: Left tibialis anterior muscle
Crystal Element: Rosette Chalcedony
Expression: Rosette Chalcedony is natural, cryptocrystalline quartz rosettes. Rosette Chalcedony highlights individual talents, promoting successful endeavours.
Message: Supernatural, intuitive, creative wisdom.
Sun Focus: You have an ability to restore balance and to rise above commonality.
Affirmation: I search for higher knowledge.

AQUARIUS 26

Birthdays: February 13th–15th

Numerology: 326
Sabian Symbol: A hydrometer
Marc Edmund Jones Key Word: Efficiency
Jane Ridder-Patrick Healing Body Point: Right fibula
Crystal Element: Vanadium Beryl
Expression: Vanadium Beryl is a light green mineral gemstone. Vanadium Beryl promotes prosperity, knowingness, growth and harmony.
Message: Comprehensive skill, energy, focus, success.
Sun Focus: You are a communication expert, summarising and expressing ideas succinctly.
Affirmation: I successfully complete what I set out to achieve.

AQUARIUS 27

Birthdays: February 14th-16th

Numerology: 327

Sabian Symbol: An ancient pottery bowl filled with violets

Marc Edmund Jones Key Word: Tradition

Jane Ridder-Patrick Healing Body Point: Left fibula

Crystal Element: Lavender Sapphire

Expression: Lavender Sapphire is natural, lilac-purple corundum. Lavender Sapphire enhances watchfulness, faithfulness and love.

Message: Practical and esoteric bonds perpetuate central beliefs.

Sun Focus: You understand the value of the past, and use it wisely in the present.

Affirmation: I learn from the past, as I grow into the future.

AQUARIUS 28

Birthdays: February 15th-17th

Numerology: 328

Sabian Symbol: A tree felled and sawed ensures a supply of wood for winter.

Marc Edmund Jones Key Word: Immediacy

Jane Ridder-Patrick Healing Body Point: Right tibia

Crystal Element: Buddstone (Quartz)

Expression: Buddstone is a green, silica-rich, African rock. Buddstone fosters spiritual acceptance, understanding, surrender and hope.

Message: Empowering impulses, discerning leadership, immediate action.

Sun Focus: You translate obscure and perplexing perceptions into simple, practical concepts.

Affirmation: I will look after my physical needs today and into the future.

AQUARIUS 29
Birthdays: February 16th-18th

Numerology: 329

Sabian Symbol: A butterfly emerging from a chrysalis

Marc Edmund Jones Key Word: Emanation

Jane Ridder-Patrick Healing Body Point: Left tibia

Crystal Element: Labradorite

Expression: Labradorite is a calcium-rich plagioclase displaying a colourful shiller. Labradorite promotes emotional and spiritual awakening, joy and wonder.

Message: Metamorphosis, growth, movement, accomplishment.

Sun Focus: You dissolve boundaries, allowing for greater personal freedom and transformation.

Affirmation: My new life starts today.

AQUARIUS 30
Birthdays: February 17th-19th

Numerology: 330

Sabian Symbol: Moonlit fields, once Babylon, are white and blooming.

Marc Edmund Jones Key Word: Continuity

Jane Ridder-Patrick Healing Body Point: Connections in lower leg

Crystal Element: White Sapphire

Expression: White Sapphire is natural, colourless corundum. White Sapphire inspires spiritual illumination, brilliance, transcendence and compassion.

Message: Faith and power maintain the success of vast and enduring achievements.

Sun Focus: Through heightened perspective, you calmly sustain unity and grace.

Affirmation: With a view from eternity everything is in perspective.

PISCES 1
Birthdays: February 18th-19th

Numerology: 331
Sabian Symbol: A public marketplace
Marc Edmund Jones Key Word: Commerce
Jane Ridder-Patrick Healing Body Point: Right calcaneum
Crystal Element: Silver
Expression: Elemental Silver is a naturally occurring metal. Silver promotes trust, excellence, balance, and the attraction and retention of wealth. It is an alchemical metal.
Message: Efficient allocation of resources enhances the positive flow of wealth.
Sun Focus: You value everyone and everything, seeing energy exchange as vital.
Affirmation: I am prosperous in my endeavours.

PISCES 2
Birthdays: February 19th-21st

Numerology: 332
Sabian Symbol: A squirrel hiding from hunters
Marc Edmund Jones Key Word: Caution
Jane Ridder-Patrick Healing Body Point: Left calcaneum
Crystal Element: Psilomelane
Expression: Psilomelane is an important source of manganese. Psilomelane enhances self-worth and intestinal fortitude during stressful periods; promotes the will to live.
Message: Tactical expertise, skill, awareness and intuition keep me safe.
Sun Focus: You are a self-sustaining, practical person who alerts others to universal principles.
Affirmation: I exercise moderation and caution in my life.

PISCES 3
Birthdays: February 20th-22nd

Numerology: 333
Sabian Symbol: A petrified forest
Marc Edmund Jones Key Word: Survival
Jane Ridder-Patrick Healing Body Point: Nerves of right foot
Crystal Element: Petrified Wood (silicified)
Expression: Petrified Wood is silicified, fossilised wood. Petrified Wood is grounding, aids in past life memory recall, and fortifies the spirit.
Message: The human senses are fundamental; Chi is eternal.
Sun Focus: An old and wise soul with many past life memories, you teach others how to love living.
Affirmation: I choose to live life in every moment.

PISCES 4
Birthdays: February 21st-23rd

Numerology: 334
Sabian Symbol: Heavy traffic on a narrow isthmus that links seaside resorts
Marc Edmund Jones Key Word: Convergence
Jane Ridder-Patrick Healing Body Point: Nerves of left foot
Crystal Element: Ocean Jasper
Expression: Ocean Jasper is a silica-rich, orbicular rock from Madagascar. Ocean Jasper focuses information, allowing life patterns and intuitive awareness to flow.
Message: The coming together of people, emotions, plans and phenomena.
Sun Focus: You are a professional helper – comforting people is what you do best.
Affirmation: I help others reach their goals, with compassion.

PISCES 5
Birthdays: February 22nd-24th

Numerology: 335
Sabian Symbol: A church bazaar
Marc Edmund Jones Key Word: Benefit
Jane Ridder-Patrick Healing Body Point: Right cuboid bone
Crystal Element: Green Kyanite
Expression: Green Kyanite is a metamorphic, aluminium silicate. Green Kyanite supports kindness, tolerance, prosperity and solidarity.
Message: Cooperatively achieving spiritual and creative success.
Sun Focus: You are an active volunteer, bringing significant social and economic value to the community.
Affirmation: Charity is divinely received into my soul, and I share it with others.

PISCES 6
Birthdays: February 23rd-25th

Numerology: 336
Sabian Symbol: Officers on dress parade
Marc Edmund Jones Key Word: Discipline
Jane Ridder-Patrick Healing Body Point: Left cuboid bone
Crystal Element: Sardonyx
Expression: Sardonyx is a white and brownish-red, banded, cryptocrystalline quartz. Sardonyx promotes self-control, mindfulness and conscientiousness.
Message: Exalted standards, obedience, dignity and loyalty.
Sun Focus: Your sense of duty, honour, respect and high ideals motivate greatness.
Affirmation: I look to my guides for help along my spiritual path.

PISCES 7

Birthdays: February 24th–26th

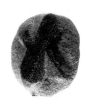

Numerology: 337
Sabian Symbol: A cross lying on rocks
Marc Edmund Jones Key Word: Conscience
Jane Ridder-Patrick Healing Body Point: Right talus
Crystal Element: Staurolite
Expression: Staurolite is a metamorphic mineral with twinned crystals forming the shape of a cross. Staurolite connects the physical and the spiritual realms.
Message: Symbols, belief systems, rituals and morals hold powerful truths.
Sun Focus: You understand that both man 'made' religion and universal spirit are valid and potent.
Affirmation: I am consciously aware.

PISCES 8

Birthdays: February 25th–27th

Numerology: 338
Sabian Symbol: A girl blowing a bugle
Marc Edmund Jones Key Word: Summons
Jane Ridder-Patrick Healing Body Point: Left talus
Crystal Element: Blue Kyanite
Expression: Blue Kyanite is a metamorphic, aluminium silicate mineral. Blue Kyanite promotes articulate, truthful and confident communication.
Message: Announced messages signal action.
Sun Focus: You show others how the power of the voice – the air and the vibration –holds magical power.
Affirmation: I speak honestly and clearly, and people take notice of me.

PISCES 9

Birthdays: February 26th–28th

Numerology: 339
Sabian Symbol: A jockey and his horse racing at great speed
Marc Edmund Jones Key Word: Practice
Jane Ridder-Patrick Healing Body Point: Right metatarsals
Crystal Element: Yellow Jasper
Expression: Yellow Jasper is an opaque variety of coloured quartz. Yellow Jasper promotes stamina, perseverance and focus, helping to defy the odds.
Message: A vital energy force moves with great speed through space and time.
Sun Focus: You have high ideals, light-speed intuition, and you will rise to meet any circumstance.
Affirmation: I move in one swift quantum leap with mind, body and spirit.

PISCES 10

Birthdays: February 27th–29th

Numerology: 340
Sabian Symbol: An aviator in the clouds
Marc Edmund Jones Key Word: Observation
Jane Ridder-Patrick Healing Body Point: Left metatarsals
Crystal Element: Scolecite
Expression: Scolecite is a zeolite with delicate sprays of acicular crystals. Scolecite promotes objectivity in progressive and group orientated activities; elemental air energy.
Message: Transcend the mundane; show others the way.
Sun Focus: In your life, you explore freedom, form, perspective, rules and the unlearning of rules.
Affirmation: Eternal perception clarifies my ideas in the now.

PISCES 11

Birthdays: February 28th–March 1st

Numerology: 341

Sabian Symbol: Men seeking illumination

Marc Edmund Jones Key Word: Dedication

Jane Ridder-Patrick Healing Body Point: Lymph vessels of foot

Crystal Element: Shiva-Lingham

Expression: Shiva-Lingham is a two-toned, cryptocrystalline quartz found in India. Shiva-Lingham stones enhance awareness of cosmic forces, leading to enlightenment.

Message: Unbiased, astute, flowing, balancing, penetrating love.

Sun Focus: Radiating timeless wisdom, you meditate and focus on receiving Divine revelations.

Affirmation: I look to the light even in my darkest moments.

PISCES 12

Birthdays: March 1st–3rd

Numerology: 342

Sabian Symbol: An examination of initiates

Marc Edmund Jones Key Word: Qualification

Jane Ridder-Patrick Healing Body Point: Plantar artery of right foot

Crystal Element: Yttrian Fluorite

Expression: Yttrian Fluorite is yttrian-rich fluorite. Yttrian Fluorite promotes success during demanding and exacting times; a stone for philosophers and students.

Message: Perform strongly and gain entrance to the higher ranks.

Sun Focus: You are a good judge of character and display the highest of ideals.

Affirmation: My trials and successes lead the way for the betterment of others.

PISCES 13

Birthdays: March 2nd–4th

Numerology: 343
Sabian Symbol: A sword in a museum
Marc Edmund Jones Key Word: Example
Jane Ridder-Patrick Healing Body Point: Plantar artery of
  left foot
Crystal Element: Iron
Expression: Iron is naturally found as an alloy of iron and nickel. Iron promotes self-belief, self-assertion and individuality.
Message: Modelling fairness, strength, compassion, determination and devotion.
Sun Focus: You find yourself in leadership positions, a model of prestige, authority and distinction.
Affirmation: I believe in the power of nonviolence.

PISCES 14

Birthdays: March 3rd–5th

Numerology: 344
Sabian Symbol: A lady in fox fur
Marc Edmund Jones Key Word: Tastefulness
Jane Ridder-Patrick Healing Body Point: Right cutaneous
  veins
Crystal Element: Yellow Diamond
Expression: Yellow Diamonds are also known as fancy coloured diamonds.
  Yellow Diamonds promote wealth, natural beauty, determination and ambition.
Message: Delightful expression, wonderful style, attention and brilliance.
Sun Focus: Elegant and refined, you express yourself in a dynamic fashion.
Affirmation: When I look good I feel great.

)(

PISCES 15

Birthdays: March 4th-6th

Numerology: 345

Sabian Symbol: An officer preparing to drill his men

Marc Edmund Jones Key Word: Preciseness

Jane Ridder-Patrick Healing Body Point: Left cutaneous
veins

Crystal Element: Andalusite

Expression: Andalusite is a cognac-coloured, pleochroic mineral. Andalusite
promotes memory recall, order and efficiency, and gallantry.

Message: Discipline and order promote the extension of civilizations.

Sun Focus: You rely on factual knowledge, knowing that accuracy is essential for
putting your point across.

Affirmation: I prepare for important events in my life.

PISCES 16

Birthdays: March 5th-7th

Numerology: 346

Sabian Symbol: The flow of inspiration

Marc Edmund Jones Key Word: Ingenuity

Jane Ridder-Patrick Healing Body Point: Cruciate
ligaments of right foot

Crystal Element: Aquamarine

Expression: Aquamarine is a blue variety of beryl. Aquamarine fosters sincerity,
security, peace of mind, happiness, understanding and love.

Message: Original and resourceful, intuitive and imaginative.

Sun Focus: Insightful, you are ahead of your time in ideas and opinions. Your
creativity is inspirational.

Affirmation: I am open and receptive to light and love.

PISCES 17
Birthdays: March 6th-8th

Numerology: 347
Sabian Symbol: An Easter promenade
Marc Edmund Jones Key Word: Celebration
Jane Ridder-Patrick Healing Body Point: Cruciate ligaments of left foot
Crystal Element: Yellow Apatite
Expression: Yellow Apatite is a phosphate mineral. Yellow Apatite promotes uplifting, cheerful, joyful, happy emotions and invites phoenix energy into your life.
Message: Exultant transformation, joyful liberation, life-filled renewal.
Sun Focus: You are versatile and flexible, a natural character actor revelling in the public arena.
Affirmation: Rejoice and be glad; today is a wonderful day.

PISCES 18
Birthdays: March 7th-9th

Numerology: 348
Sabian Symbol: In a gigantic tent a spectacular performance is underway.
Marc Edmund Jones Key Word: Apportionment
Jane Ridder-Patrick Healing Body Point: Extensor muscles of right toes
Crystal Element: Stilbite
Expression: Stilbite is a secondary zeolite mineral. Stilbite creates a loving, clear space for self-expression and psychic development.
Message: Empower, intensify and inspire through extravagant revelations.
Sun Focus: A gifted performer and a great teacher, you inspire and motivate people.
Affirmation: I am enchanting, exhilarating and unforgettable.

PISCES 19

Birthdays: March 8th-10th

Numerology: 349

Sabian Symbol: A master instructing his pupil

Marc Edmund Jones Key Word: Elucidation

Jane Ridder-Patrick Healing Body Point: Extensor muscles of left toes

Crystal Element: Benitoite

Expression: Benitoite is typically a blue, barium, titanium silicate. Benitoite enhances the synthesis of information into understanding; allows access to the akashic records.

Message: Communication of higher knowledge, wisdom and love.

Sun Focus: You clarify problematic issues, empowering people towards successful resolutions.

Affirmation: I see beyond eyesight; I understand more than I hear.

PISCES 20

Birthdays: March 9th-11th

Numerology: 350

Sabian Symbol: A table set for an evening meal

Marc Edmund Jones Key Word: Familiarity

Jane Ridder-Patrick Healing Body Point: Right fibula muscle

Crystal Element: Pewter

Expression: Pewter is a metallic alloy of tin and lead. Pewter supports a balanced appetite, positive conversation and family harmony.

Message: Sustaining emotional nourishment, comfortable and friendly.

Sun Focus: You are a friendly, hospitable person; you make people feel special and comfortable.

Affirmation: I support healthy and bountiful nutrition for my mind, body and soul.

PISCES 21

Birthdays: March 10th-12th

Numerology: 351

Sabian Symbol: A little white lamb, a child, and a Chinese servant.

Marc Edmund Jones Key Word: Talent

Jane Ridder-Patrick Healing Body Point: Left fibula muscle

Crystal Element: Zircon

Expression: Zircon, or Zirconium silicate, is a natural mineral specimen. Zircon fortifies a sense of purpose and of belonging in life, and enhances innate and divine gifts.

Message: Sense of character, purpose in life, motivation and genius.

Sun Focus: You are drawn to vocations that require self-sacrifice and have clear, positive social impact.

Affirmation: I make the most of my natural abilities.

PISCES 22

Birthdays: March 11th-13th

Numerology: 352

Sabian Symbol: A man bringing down the new law from Sinai

Marc Edmund Jones Key Word: Mandate

Jane Ridder-Patrick Healing Body Point: Achilles tendon of right foot

Crystal Element: Platinum

Expression: Platinum is a valuable white metal. Platinum acts as a catalyst integrating new concepts and ideas into reality; it enhances flexibility and endurance.

Message: Facilitate the integration of Divine principles; advance the ascension process.

Sun Focus: You present to the world revelations of spirit, formulating new theories and actualities.

Affirmation: I accept that universal law changes with heightened perspective.

PISCES 23

Birthdays: March 12th-14th

Numerology: 353
Sabian Symbol: A materialising medium
Marc Edmund Jones Key Word: Sensitivity
Jane Ridder-Patrick Healing Body Point: Achilles tendon of
  left foot
Crystal Element: Pallasite
Expression: Pallasite is a stony, iron meteorite. Pallasite enhances psychic
  channelling, practical insights, and the ability to clearly receive and clarify
  messages.
Message: Privy to spiritual energy, messages, empathy, sensitivity.
Sun Focus: You have a true sense of kindness and compassion; you mirror the
  energy around you.
Affirmation: I am a channel for enlightened messages.

PISCES 24

Birthdays: March 13th-15th

Numerology: 354
Sabian Symbol: An inhabited island
Marc Edmund Jones Key Word: Cultivation
Jane Ridder-Patrick Healing Body Point: Right distal
  tibio-fibular joint
Crystal Element: Dolomite
Expression: Dolomite is a sedimentary, calcium, magnesium carbonate.
  Dolomite promotes a belief in Divine order and karmic balance.
Message: Tolerance, communal harmony, group attention and focus.
Sun Focus: Working with the hopes and ambitions of others, you support
  successful coexistence.
Affirmation: I devote time and thought to manifesting positive outcomes in my
  life.

PISCES 25

Birthdays: March 14th-16th

Numerology: 355

Sabian Symbol: The purging of the priesthood

Marc Edmund Jones Key Word: Reformation

Jane Ridder-Patrick Healing Body Point: Left distal tibio-fibular joint

Crystal Element: Chiastolite

Expression: Chiastolite, also known as Cross Stone, is a variety of andalusite. Chiastolite promotes harmony, understanding during restructuring, and also aids in astral travel.

Message: Transform, purify, revive, breathe new life into and renew spiritual focus.

Sun Focus: Respectful, trustworthy and dependable, people look to you as a powerful mediator.

Affirmation: I acknowledge my faults and I endeavour to return to a rightful course.

PISCES 26

Birthdays: March 15th-17th.

Numerology: 356

Sabian Symbol: A new moon that divides its influences

Marc Edmund Jones Key Word: Finesse

Jane Ridder-Patrick Healing Body Point: Plantar nerves

Crystal Element: Selenite

Expression: Selenite is a colourless, pearl-like, transparent gypsum. Selenite supports prosperous new beginnings and the manifesting of ability, and refines psychic talent.

Message: Increasing grace, harmony, balance and beauty.

Sun Focus: You are fond of art, music, and refined culture; you promote a well-balanced lifestyle.

Affirmation: I use new moon energy to create a new vision for myself and my life.

PISCES 27

Birthdays: March 16th-18th

Numerology: 357
Sabian Symbol: A harvest moon
Marc Edmund Jones Key Word: Benediction
Jane Ridder-Patrick Healing Body Point: Phalanges of right foot
Crystal Element: Carnelian
Expression: Carnelian is a brownish orange, translucent, cryptocrystalline quartz. Carnelian awakens self-wisdom and promotes self-expression.
Message: Gratefully sharing bountiful gifts; festivity and reunion.
Sun Focus: Gregarious, sociable and generous, you build healthy and enduring relationships.
Affirmation: I rejoice in the many gifts with which I am blessed.

PISCES 28

Birthdays: March 17th-19th

Numerology: 358
Sabian Symbol: A fertile garden under the full moon
Marc Edmund Jones Key Word: Ultimacy
Jane Ridder-Patrick Healing Body Point: Phalanges of left foot
Crystal Element: Rainbow Moonstone
Expression: Rainbow Moonstone is colourful Labradorite Feldspar. Rainbow Moonstone enhances natural abilities, and encourages transformation, strength and love.
Message: Absolute unconditional love – the ultimate view.
Sun Focus: You spread tranquillity, comfort and love, and share your prosperity with others.
Affirmation: Enlightened purpose, quality and intention are important to me.

PISCES 29

Birthdays: March 18th-20th

Numerology: 359

Sabian Symbol: Light breaking into a rainbow as it passes through a prism

Marc Edmund Jones Key Word: Validation

Jane Ridder-Patrick Healing Body Point: Toenails of right foot

Crystal Element: Natural Glass (silica)

Expression: Natural Glass can be created by lightning strikes or meteor impacts. Glass merges earth, air, fire and water; focuses light, and carries information.

Message: The precise quality is uncovered, ensuring a simple interpretation.

Sun Focus: You clarify complex issues by verifying concisely and clearly the key elements involved.

Affirmation: I endorse happiness, diversity, inclusiveness and hope.

PISCES 30

Birthdays: March 20th- 21st

Numerology: 360

Sabian Symbol: The Great Stone Face

Marc Edmund Jones Key Word: Discernment

Jane Ridder-Patrick Healing Body Point: Toenails of left foot

Crystal Element: Gneiss

Expression: Gneiss is a banded, metamorphic stone. Gneiss promotes a strong sense of self and enhances collective understanding of cause and effect.

Message: Advanced metamorphosis, intense experience, total transformation.

Sun Focus: Through visualisation and interpretation, you reflect universal principles and embody strength.

Affirmation: I project the image of the person I want to be.

Acknowledgements and Thanks

First and foremost, my deep love and gratitude to Ross, Harry, Ben, and my mum Doris for their unconditional support, practical assistance and love – thank you.

My heartfelt thanks goes to:

Everyone at Earthdancer, in particular my publisher, Arwen Lentz, who was motivating and patient when I needed it the most.

Thierry Bogliolo and everyone at Findhorn Press for supporting me in my quest to publish *Crystal Astrology*.

Claudine Bloomfield for her expertise and skill in the editing process.

Michael Gienger for his intelligent contributions during the construction phase of the book.

Aurora Press for providing permission to utilise Dr. Marc Edmund Jones' Sabian Symbols key words.

Jane Ridder-Patrick, astrologer, and author of *A Handbook to Medical Astrology*, for providing permission to utilise the list of body parts.

Lynda Hill, astrologer, author, and dear friend (www.sabiansymbols.com), for her inspirational work, her enthusiasm, teachings and friendship.

Radu Moisoiu (www.astrologyweekly.com) for his generosity and skill in creating www.crystalastrology.com.

Huette and Julie Thomson at Awesome Universe (www.awesomeuniverse.com) for providing me that safe, first step into writing.

Kellie the Crystal Deva of Avalon Crystals™ (www.neatstuff.net/avalon) for her generosity with Avalonite – photos, definitions and specimens.

Linda Johnson for the photograph of Yttrian Fluorite (www.newage.com.au and www.crystalshop.com.au).

Brynna Scherloum of S&A Beads (Beadstore.com) for the photograph of Bauxite, and everyone at www.geodiscoveries.com.au for their mineralogical expertise.

Extra special thanks and blessings go to Ruth, Jean, Mary, Barbara, Danuta, Mark, Judith, Estelle, Doug, Deleece, Robyn, Marilyn, Deb, Elise, Rob, Lisa, Gail, Georgia, Carrol, Alyssa, James, Benny, Luke, Jack, Karys, Steve, Sean, and all my friends – you help crystallise my life.

Bibliography

Original Work References

With kind permission of Jane Ridder-Patrick, 29 East London Street, Edinburgh EH7 4 BN, Scotland, www.janeridderpatrick.com, we have used her translation of the Ebertin Degree Areas, listed in the astrology chapters under: *Jane Ridder-Patrick Healing Body Point*; they are reprinted from: *A Handbook of Medical Astrology* by Jane Ridder-Patrick, published by CrabApple Press, Edinburgh 2006, ISBN 978-0-9551989-0-8

With Kind permission of Aurora Press, PO Box 573, Santa Fe, NM 87504, www.aurorapress.com, we have used the Dr. Marc Edmund Jones Keywords in the astrology chapters under: *Marc Edmund Jones Key Word*, they are reprinted from: *The Sabian Symbols In Astrology*, by Dr. Marc Edmund Jones, ISBN: 978-0-943358-40-6

Illustration Credits

© Ines Blersch, www.inesblersch.de: all other photographs.
© Marina Costelloe: Fulgurite p. 53, Clay (Kaolinite) p. 60, Rose Gold p. 92, Peacock Ore (Bornite) p. 67, Aqua Aura p. 112, Atacamite p. 112, Crocoite p. 120, Okenite/Mesolite p. 199, Graphite p. 189, Pewter p. 212.
© Stephen Coburn, Fotolia, www.fotolia.de, picture of: Pink Diamond p. 191.
© Kellie JO Conn, the crystal deva, www.avaloncrystals.com, picture of: Avalonite p. 93 and we specially credit her for discovery of the avalonite.
© Marc Dietrich, Fotolia, www.fotolia.de, picture of: Blue Diamond p. 148.
© Linda Johnson, www.newage.com.au and www.crystalshop.com.au, picture of: Yttrian Fluorite p. 208.
© Michael Kempf, Fotolia, www.fotolia.de, picture of: White Gold ring p. 113.
© Dipl. Ing. Heinrich Pniok, www.pse-mendelejew.de, pictures of: Tin p. 77, Nickel p. 81, Iron p. 209, Platinum p. 213.

© Brynna Scherloum, S&A Beads, www.beadstore.com, picture of: Bauxite p.59
© Karola Siebert, www.makrogalerie.de, pictures of: Agatized Dinosaur Bone p.45, Faceted White Diamond p.48, Colourless Spinel p.53, Goldstone p.54, Mother of Pearl p.59, Jacinth (orange zircon) p.61, Olivine p.62, Limestone p.71, Cubic Zirconia p.73, Tanzanite p.74, Siberian Quartz p.79, Pumice p.86, Bismuth p.90, Magnetite p.95, Sinhalite p.95, Green Spinel p.98, Violane p.108, Freshwater Pearls p.116, Euclase p.177, Black Marble p.125, Wollastonite p.126, Black Spinel p.126, Violet Spinel p.137, Pearl (ocean) p.146, Yellow Sapphire p.162, Granite p.179, Phenacite p.193, Lavender Sapphire p.201, White Sapphire p.202, Silver (native) p.203, Yellow Diamond p.209, Benitoite p.212.
© David Smith, Fotolia, www.fotolia.de, picture of Sand p.150
© Andy Stucki, Siber+Siber AG, www.siber-siber.ch, picture of Gold in Quarz p.145
© Zauberhut, Fotolia, www.fotolia.de, picture of: Seashells p.138

Additionally our thanks go to the company Edelsteinschleiferei Gustav Zhang for the kind loan of the crystals sinhalite and green spinell for photography. www.gustavzang.de

Index of Crystal Names

All the important information about 430 healing gemstones in a neat pocket-book! Michael Gienger, known for his popular introductory work 'Crystal Power, Crystal Healing', here presents a comprehensive directory of all the gemstones currently in use. In a clear, concise and precise style, with pictures accompanying the text, the author describes the characteristics and healing functions of each crystal.

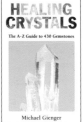

Michael Gienger
Healing Crystals
The A - Z Guide to 430 Gemstones
Paperback, 96 pages
ISBN 978-1-84409-067-9

This is an easy-to-use A-Z guide for treating many common ailments and illnesses with the help of crystal therapy. It includes a comprehensive colour appendix with photographs and short descriptions of each gemstone recommended.

Michael Gienger
The Healing Crystals First Aid Manual
A Practical A to Z of Common Ailments and Illnesses and How They Can Be Best Treated with Crystal Therapy
288 pages, with 16 colour plates
ISBN 978-1-84409-084-6

For further information and book catalogue contact:
Findhorn Press, 305a The Park, Forres IV36 3TE, Scotland.
Earthdancer Books is an Imprint of Findhorn Press.

tel +44 (0)1309-690582   fax +44 (0)1309-690036

info@findhornpress.com   www.findhornpress.com   www.earthdancer.co.uk

EARTHDANCER

A FINDHORN PRESS IMPRINT